Fannie Flagg's Original Whistle Stop Cafe Cookbook

Fannie Flagg's Original

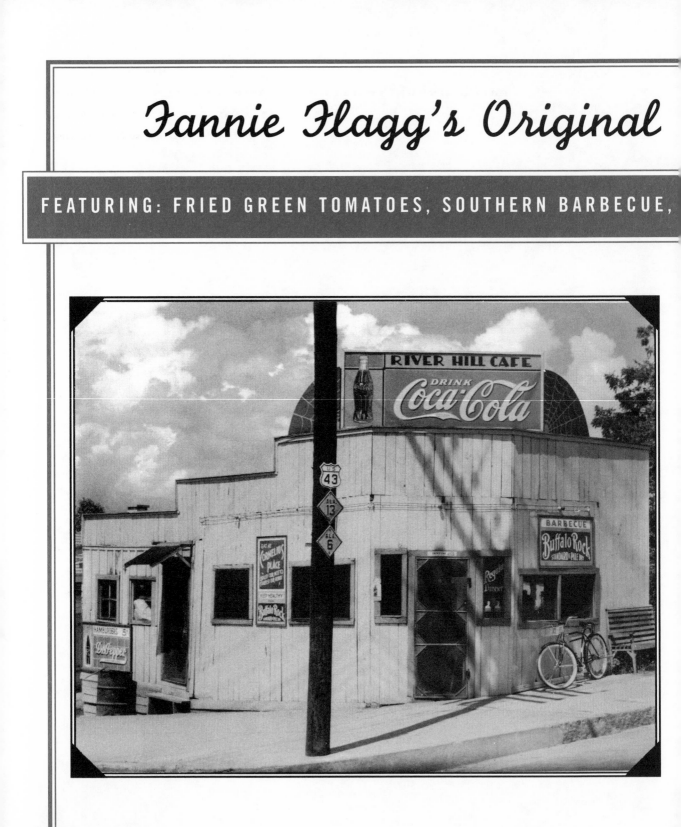

Whistlestop Cafe Cookbook

BANANA SPLIT CAKE, AND MANY OTHER GREAT RECIPES

by Fannie Flagg

with recipes from

**THE
IRONDALE
CAFE**

**Fawcett Columbine
New York**

A Fawcett Columbine Book
Published by Ballantine Books

Copyright © 1993 by Fannie Flagg

Illustrations copyright © 1993 by Judy Soderquist Cummins

All rights reserved under International and Pan-American Copyright Conventions.
Published in the United States by Ballantine Books,
a division of Random House, Inc., New York,
and simultaneously in Canada by Random House of Canada Limited, Toronto.

Excerpts from *Fried Green Tomatoes at the Whistle Stop Cafe* by Fannie Flagg copyright © 1987 by Fannie Flagg. Reprinted by permission of Random House, Inc.

Library of Congress Catalog Card Number: 95-90148
ISBN: 0-449-91028-8

Cover design by Barbara Leff
Cover illustration by Dan Brown

Manufactured in the United States of America
First Ballantine Books Trade Paperback Edition: September 1995

12 13 14 15 16 17 18 19 20

Aunt Bess couldn't resist feeding anybody.

This book is dedicated to the memory of my Aunt Bess.
It was in her cafe that I first learned about good food and kindness,
two things I still treasure.

Acknowledgments

First and foremost I must again thank the wonderful McMichael family, owners of the original cafe in Irondale, Alabama, for all their generosity and help in making this book possible. Special thanks to Debbie Maugans who worked tirelessly on the recipes. Thanks also to my other Birmingham, Alabama friends, Norma Warren and Ann Harvey for their help. Also, many thanks to my good friend and photo researcher for this book, Jo Roy Donaldson, and her research assistants, Leslie Thompson and Michelle Andrews. Also, thank you to the following for their assistance in photo research: Don Veasey, Dr. Marvin Whiting, Jim Murray, George Ewert, Elisa Baldwin, Mike Thomason, Tanya Zanish, Del Wilson, Gail Miller DeLoach, Jerry Cotten, Nancy Bounds, Elaine Owens, Petie Bogen-Garrett, Deborah Evans, Kathryn Tucker Windam, Donna L. Newton.

Many thanks to my wonderful agent and friend, Wendy Weil, and to my Ballantine editor Ginny Faber and her assistant, Phebe Kirkham, who were both a joy to work with. Last but not least I wish to gratefully acknowledge my beloved Random House editor Sam Vaughan, who thankfully oversees every word I write and earns his unofficial title of "the nicest man in publishing" every day. His encouragement and support are the two balloons that have kept me, and continue to keep me, afloat.

Contents

Preface

"*A* cookbook! Why in the world are *you* of all people going to write a cookbook?" That was the response when I told my friends what I was doing. You would have thought that I had just announced my attempt to overthrow a foreign government with a fork. "Why not?" I asked somewhat defensively, considering that most of them had been to my home for dinner. I turned to my friend. "Mickey, how can you say that? Why just the other night your very own husband, Bob, just raved and raved about my pork chops and black-eyed peas!" She paused. "Now, Fannie, I didn't say they weren't good; it's just that they are the only thing you ever serve."

"That's not true," I cried. "Remember the year before last when I had the pork chops and turnip greens instead?"

Anyway, I guess by now you can pretty much get the picture. My culinary skills are somewhat limited. To tell you the truth, I was surprised myself when my publisher called. "A *cookbook*! . . . Why in the world would you want *me* of all people to do a cookbook?"

Then I thought, Hey, wait a minute . . . why *not* me? After all, doesn't my relationship with food go way back? But then, whose doesn't? But I am a Southerner and everyone knows we have all been preoccupied with food and stories since birth. Me, perhaps, more than most. I have always loved to eat, loved to be around other people eating; why I even love to see *pictures* of people eating. Besides, I have written two entire novels, both of which revolve around restaurants, one a malt shop and one a cafe. So, why not me indeed?

As the only child of a mother who did not like to cook, I have eaten out almost every day of my life and enjoyed myself immensely, so I certainly know good food when I see it. Better still, when I taste it. Anyhow, they say you should only write about things that you are interested in and care about, and I certainly qualify on both counts.

So I knew right off the bat that this book would be great fun. But there was another reason I wanted to do this book. Since the

FANNIE
FLAGG'S
ORIGINAL
WHISTLE STOP
CAFE
COOKBOOK
•
2

novel and the film version of *Fried Green Tomatoes at the Whistle Stop Cafe* were released, I have received thousands of letters from sweet people all over the world, asking me if there really was a Whistle Stop Cafe. Did I have one in mind when I was writing the book, and if so could they please have some of the original recipes?

The answer is yes. There really was such a cafe. The Irondale Cafe was started by my great aunt Bess in the thirties and she ran it for over fifty years. It is located in Irondale, Alabama, a small town just outside my hometown of Birmingham. The good news is that it is thriving, doing a roaring business, with people still coming from miles around to enjoy those same hot delicious meals. Not only that, Virginia Johnson, that fabulous cook who first went to work for my aunt when she was eleven, can still be found in the kitchen, happily frying up a fresh batch of fried green tomatoes every day, the same kind that I, along with generations of others, have enjoyed since we were children. And the best news of all is that the McMichaels family, who bought the cafe from my Aunt Bess and continue to run the cafe so successfully, are dear friends and the nicest people you will ever meet.

So I am delighted to share their original recipes with you, just in case you can't make it down to Alabama anytime soon. We all want you to be able to enjoy and have the fun of making and tasting real downhome cafe cooking in your own kitchen. Not only can you fix and serve it, you can be right in style, foodwise. The marketing people tell me that these recipes fall into the category of "comfort food" that has suddenly become very In and Trendy. When I heard that, I surely had to laugh. Just think . . . I had been In and Trendy all my life and just didn't know it, because I have *always* been comfortable eating a good meal.

Which brings me to the main reason I wanted so much to write this book. Lately it seems everyone is mad at someone, with groups on every corner, on the radio, on television, screaming about something or someone or other they don't like. And there is so much anger in the air that you almost see it like a thick fog. In times like this, I think it is particularly important to try to be as calm and happy as possible. And I don't know about you, but, I have always been happiest where food was concerned. Some of the best times in my life have revolved around meals. Let's face it—eating is fun. I like everything about it. I particularly like the sounds and the smells and the friendly atmosphere. People laughing, dishes rattling, and glasses tinkling are music to my ears, and I find it impossible to be miserable and angry and enjoy a good meal at the same time. Everybody could use a little comfort these days and is there any place better for a little comfort than a cafe?

So come on back with me if you will, to a time when people were as sweet as the tea they served and everyone knew you and liked you, even knew your daddy's daddy. To a time that no matter how poor you were or what hard times you might be going through, nothing could make you feel better than a side of creamy hot mashed potatoes served with a smile. When the cafe was your home away from home, the center of town where you could always find a friend and have a laugh. Down at the cafe, where the food always tasted better than it looked and somebody was always around, morning, noon, and night, and after church on Sundays; where you had your favorite table, a place you were always welcome, as familiar as your own living room; where if they were busy, you helped yourself to more iced tea or hot coffee; where you sometimes just left your money on the counter and never counted your change.

No matter where you come from, East or West, North or South, and no matter if your cafe was called the Whistle Stop, the Busy Bee, the Melrose Diner, or the Chatter Box, close your eyes, forget your troubles, and come on back home with me for just a little while. . . .

It is sunrise. The birds are just starting to chirp, the dogs begin to shake themselves and let out a bark or two, and kitchen lights start to come on one by one all over town. There is an early morning chill in the air. But over at the cafe the kitchen is warm, the radio is playing, bacon is frying and biscuits are being cut, and the cooks are wide awake. One by one, sleepy-eyed customers stumble in the door with their newspapers and hot steaming coffee is placed in front of them by waitresses who know just how they take it, cream no sugar, sugar no cream, or just plain black. . . .

As the morning progresses the dishes slowly start to clatter and as the kitchen door opens and closes you can hear the sounds of eggs and bacon frying and the warm rich smell of fresh biscuits baking wafts through the room. The pace gets faster, more coffee is poured, eyes brighten, laughs start, and pretty soon the whole place is humming and rattling like a cage full of happy finches chirping away. And then, after a couple of hours, it slowly calms down into that soft quiet non-time between breakfast and lunch, that lull until the lunch bunch suddenly comes slammin' and bangin' in the door, once more loud and ravenous, calling out for the Blue Plate Special. . . .

FANNIE
FLAGG'S
ORIGINAL
WHISTLE STOP
CAFE
COOKBOOK
•
4

This happy scenario goes on day after day, week after week, year after year, and no matter if you wander away for a day or a decade, when you come back it is always the same over at the cafe. Like a good play that has been running for years, the cast may change a little from time to time but the storyline remains the same, feed the people with love, a smile, and good food.

And although the word *cafe* is French, I'm sure that most little lean-to shacks that have popped up all over the country would be surprised to learn of their origins. These little cafes were not always grand but they were the very heart of the town, with personalities of their own. And when one closed down it was mourned for generations. For weeks afterward, you could see lost old men still peering inside the boarded up windows, hoping that maybe, somehow, it could come back to life. Conversations start with "Remember when the cafe was still running, that time we had lunch with Memaw or supper with Uncle Buddy?" Or: "Remember when we used to have the Rotary's meeting over at the cafe?" People still can't believe it's closed and none of the new, cold, operating room sterile, orange plastic fast food joints can ever take the place of the old cafe, where the silverware never matched and more often than not was bent and covered with water spots. But still, it felt like silverware and it was silverware with a past. That spoon you are stirring your coffee with may have been used by your grandmother thirty years ago, and that knife by your first cousin just yesterday; not some flimsy white plastic "knives and forks" in a cellophane package to be thrown away. And oh, if only those old chipped plates could talk. How many faces have they looked up at through the years, how many pretty young girls have they seen grow into beautiful old women, soldier boys come and go, handsome cowlicky boys turn into grandfathers, and how many babies have they seen cry or laugh with delight? And those poor old chairs. How many times have they been kicked by children, knocked over by people in a hurry, pushed and pulled and dragged around the room, joining other tables for conversations about not much of anything, I suspect, nothing less than the everyday lives of a town full of people trying to do their best day after day, year after year.

So my hat's off to you, all you old cafes that are gone now, and to the ones still going. You made life a little easier for all of us: simple, clean, steady, and honest . . . just like a good friend.

What is Cafe Cooking?

*L*et me assure you right from the start: Cafe cooking is not hard; in fact it is nothing more than good, old-fashioned home cooking not done at home. Years ago there were few jobs for women outside the home and if a woman had to go to work, cooking was one of the few jobs she could do. So, most cafe recipes were for the same food that she cooked at home for her family, only when it was cooked at the cafe, the recipes were adjusted for larger amounts. Cafe cooking became so good because first, you didn't have to cook it; second, you didn't have to clean up afterward; and third and most important, throughout the years as cafes cooked for and served hundreds of people, and kept them coming back for more, they had the opportunity to perfect the dishes and to learn what little bits of this and that could create something that was easy, fast, and delicious.

What we have done for you here is just simply to break down these recipes to serve a smaller amount, in order to fit your family instead of a whole cafe. Because I consider myself to be somewhat of an expert on cafe cooking—God knows I have been a satisfied customer—you can rest assured that I have personally tested each and every one of these dishes for you, to make sure they are accurate, safe, and authentic. And dear reader, I have been forced to test some of these recipes over and over again—especially the ones for coconut cake and pecan pie!

It's been a rough job . . . but someone had to do it. Have fun and Good luck.

—Fannie Flagg

*W*hen I tell people about all the good recipes from the cafe, they say, "Sounds delicious. But of course you can't eat like that every day." People at the Irondale Cafe say, "Why not?"

—Fannie Flagg

"*M*y momma and Aunt Idgie ran a cafe. It wasn't nothing more than a little pine-knot affair, but I'll tell you one thing: We always ate and so did everybody else who ever came around there asking for food . . . and that was black and white. I never saw Aunt Idgie turn down a soul, and she was known to give a man a little drink if he needed it. . . ."
—Stump Threadgoode from Fried Green Tomatoes at
the Whistle Stop Cafe

*E*velyn,

Here are some of Sipsey's original recipes I wrote down. They have given me so much pleasure, I thought I'd pass them on to you, especially the one for Fried Green Tomatoes.

I love you, dear little Evelyn. Be happy. I am happy.
Your Friend,
Mrs. Cleo Threadgoode

BREAKFASTS

Dawn Breakfast of Upsilon Chapter.

Grits

*S*oon after I came up north, people used to make fun of the fact that I loved grits. They said that anybody who would eat that stuff was crazy. They would turn up their noses and look superior. I began to feel bad about myself and wondered if maybe they were right. *Then I ate some rutabaga!* Moral: People who eat rutabaga should not throw stones.

Grits. Them's fighting words. Grits separate the men from the boys, the girls from the women, and a true Southerner from the rest. Breakfast isn't the same without them, like a bride with no veil. When I first came to California I was surprised that they served fruit on the plate with bacon and eggs. I asked the waitress if they had any grits.

She looked at me. "What's a grit?" she asked.

"No, it's not one grit, it's plural grits. Just as y'all is plural, never used to refer to one person—oh never mind. Grits are little white ground up corn, cooked up and served with butter."

"Really," she said. "And you eat this?"

"Yes," I said. "Well, not only me, but a lot of people do."

"What do they taste like?"

She had me there. "Well . . . well . . . they taste like . . ."

She tried again. "Why do you like them?"

Ask most Southerners why they like grits and they will look at you baffled and confused. They don't know why a question like that was asked in the first place. Then they will scratch their heads and say, "I really don't know why . . . do you?" I guess it's the same reason I love my mother . . . I just do.

But take it from me, there is nothing better than a side of hot steaming grits swimming with sweet butter and a little salt and pepper. Now, I have been told that some people have been known to put sugar on them, perhaps confusing them with cream of wheat, which they ain't. I am horrified to hear it. But to each her own. No matter how you eat them they are wonderful, and not only are they good, they have multiple uses. I personally have used uncooked grits to put out kitchen fires, as emergency kitty litter

FANNIE
FLAGG'S
ORIGINAL
WHISTLE STOP
CAFE
COOKBOOK
•
10

(for a Southern cat), killed fire ants with them, wrapped grits in cheesecloth and put them in my closets to absorb moisture, used them as little mounds of fake snow in Christmas mangers.

Grits

3¾ cups water (or half milk and half water)
¾ teaspoon salt
¾ cup regular grits, uncooked

Bring water to a boil in a large saucepan; stir in salt. Gradually pour in grits, stirring constantly. Cover; reduce heat to low, and cook 10 minutes or until thick, stirring occasionally. Serve hot with butter, if desired.   **YIELD: 4 SERVINGS**

Cheese Grits

These are wonderful to serve with ham, pork chops or just about any other dish. So, next time you find yourself reaching for the same old boring rice or potatoes, cook up a pot of cheese grits instead.

4 cups water
½ teaspoon salt
1 cup uncooked regular grits
½ cup butter or margarine
1 6-ounce roll processed cheese food with garlic, or 6 ounces Velveeta cheese
1 cup (4 ounces) shredded Colby cheese
3 eggs, beaten

Preheat oven to 350° F. Bring water to a boil in a large saucepan, add salt, and gradually stir in grits. Cover, reduce heat, and simmer until very thick, stirring occasionally (about 10 to 15 minutes). Add butter, processed cheese, and ½ cup shredded

FANNIE
FLAGG'S
ORIGINAL
WHISTLE STOP
CAFE
COOKBOOK
•
12

Colby cheese; stir until melted. Remove from heat. Quickly stir ⅓ cup hot mixture into eggs; add to remaining hot grits, stirring constantly. Pour into a lightly greased 1¾-quart baking dish and bake for 55 minutes. Sprinkle with remaining ½ cup Colby cheese and bake 5 more minutes. **YIELD: 6 TO 8 SERVINGS**

Attention: There is a man out there named Noel who was visiting Birmingham in June of 1961. I attempted to make a bowl of cheese grits for him. I was told that shortly afterward he was taken to the hospital suffering from a blocked intestine. Noel dear, if you read this, call me. I think I know what I did wrong.

FANNIE
FLAGG'S
ORIGINAL
WHISTLESTOP
CAFE
COOKBOOK

•

14

Waffles

Stir in ⅓ cup finely chopped pecans before cooking, if you like protein. These are "lite" and delicious with a good maple syrup to hold them together.

2	eggs
1¼	cups buttermilk
¼	teaspoon baking soda
½	cup vegetable oil
1	tablespoon sugar
1¾	cups self-rising flour

Grease and heat a waffle iron. Beat eggs in mixing bowl; add buttermilk, soda, oil, and sugar; mix well with a wire whisk. Add flour; whisk until smooth. Pour batter into waffle iron and bake until steaming stops and waffles are light brown.   YIELD: TWELVE 4-INCH WAFFLES

The coffee club—every cafe has one—consists usually of all the older men in town. They gather in the cafe at six in the morning for their coffee and visit with each other to catch up on the latest. Most of these guys have been doing this every day for thirty years or more—they discuss what's going on in their town, their state, the country, and straighten out the world. I am pleased to be an honorary coffee club member in my hometown in Alabama, and I'll tell you there is no better place to get the word. *Forget* newspapers, TV, radio: To find out what's *really* happening, which way the wind's blowing, I go down to the cafe and listen. There are several lifetimes of wisdom sitting there, as there are all over the country. Join them sometime. You'll soon know more than Dan Rather.

Buttermilk Pancakes

2　eggs
¼　cup vegetable oil or melted butter
2　cups buttermilk
1　tablespoon sugar
2　teaspoons baking powder
½　teaspoon baking soda
½　teaspoon salt
1　cup all-purpose flour
¾　cup self-rising cornmeal

Beat eggs in a large bowl; beat in remaining ingredients in order, mixing until smooth. For each pancake, pour about ¼ cup batter onto a hot, lightly greased griddle. Turn pancakes when tops are covered with bubbles, and cook the other side. Serve with syrup or hot jam.　**YIELD: ABOUT SIXTEEN 4-INCH PANCAKES**

*B*LUE *P*LATE *S*PECIALS

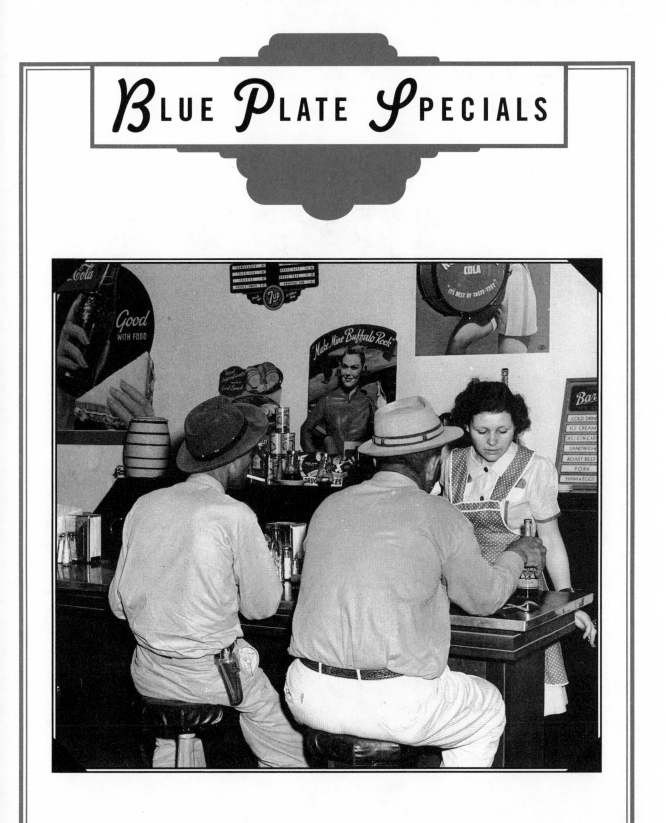

The Beloved Bird

*A*ll Southerners love poultry—chicken, turkey, quail. It is said we will eat anything with wings on it. Once, when I was a child, I heard of a family that actually tried to cook up the feather duster!

FANNIE
FLAGG'S
ORIGINAL
WHISTLE STOP
CAFE
COOKBOOK
•
18

Fried Chicken Livers

There is nothing better than fresh chicken livers. I eat them for breakfast with eggs. They are great to put in omelettes. I like them with onions too.

    1   **pound chicken livers**
    1   **cup buttermilk**
    1   **cup self-rising flour**
    Vegetable oil

Combine livers and buttermilk and let stand 10 minutes. Drain in a colander; dredge livers in flour. Deep-fry in hot oil (350° F.) for 3 to 4 minutes, or until browned. Drain.

YIELD: 4 SERVINGS

You must remember that the South was once defeated in war. It hurt our feelings. So you must forgive us if we are prone to brag a bit about our football teams, our pretty girls, and our food. After all, fair is fair. . . .

FANNIE
FLAGG'S
ORIGINAL
WHISTLE STOP
CAFE
COOKBOOK
•
20

Creamed Chicken

If the gravy is too thick for you, add a little water to thin it and simmer 1 minute.

> ¼   cup butter or margarine
> ½   cup thinly sliced celery
> ¼   cup self-rising flour
> 1½ cups milk
> ½   teaspoon salt
> Dash of pepper
> Dash of red pepper
>   2   cups diced cooked chicken
>   3   large biscuits or 3 large slices dry toast, split

Melt butter in a small saucepan over medium-low heat; add celery. Cover and cook until tender. Sprinkle flour over mixture and stir until smooth. Cook 1 minute, stirring constantly. Gradually stir in milk until smooth; add salt, pepper, red pepper, and chicken. Cook, stirring constantly, until thickened. Serve over biscuits or toast.   **YIELD: 3 SERVINGS**

My granddaddy used to play checkers with his old rooster and the rooster usually won. Is it any wonder I have so much respect for chicken? Chicken chicken chicken, oh how I love chicken . . . you can fry it . . . you can bake it . . . you can steam it . . . you can boil it . . . you can grill it . . . you can serve it with dumplings, serve it with rice, make soup or croquettes or pot pies out of it. Is there anything *better*? The best seller at any cafe is always the chicken, and I think the reason it's always so good is that they sell so much of it and it's always fresh.

Chicken Croquettes

3 tablespoons butter or margarine

3 tablespoons all-purpose flour, plus extra for dredging

½ cup plus 1 tablespoon milk

¼ teaspoon salt

¼ teaspoon pepper

½ cup mayonnaise

2 cups minced cooked chicken

1 egg, beaten

1 cup finely crushed saltine cracker crumbs

Melt butter in a heavy saucepan over low heat; add 3 tablespoons flour, stirring until smooth. Cook 1 minute, stirring constantly. Gradually add ½ cup milk; cook over medium heat, stirring constantly, until mixture leaves side of pan. Stir in salt and pepper. Remove from heat; stir in mayonnaise and chicken. Cover and chill 1 hour.

Shape chicken mixture into 6 balls or logs. Combine egg and 1 tablespoon milk, mixing well. Dredge croquettes in flour, dip in egg mixture, and roll in cracker crumbs. Deep-fry, a few at a time, in hot oil (370° F.) for 3 to 5 minutes, or until golden brown. Drain on paper towels. **YIELD: 6 SERVINGS**

FANNIE
FLAGG'S
ORIGINAL
WHISTLE STOP
CAFE
COOKBOOK

•

22

Skinless Fried Chicken

I love to serve Fried Chicken with biscuits and honey!

8 chicken breast halves
Salt
Ice water
2 cups buttermilk
2 to 3 cups self-rising flour
Vegetable oil

Remove skin from chicken breast halves. Place them in a large container with a cover; pour salted ice water over chicken, covering completely (use about 2 teaspoons salt per quart of water). Cover and refrigerate overnight.

Up to 2 hours before cooking, drain chicken and pat dry. Place in a large bowl. Pour buttermilk over chicken and refrigerate until time to fry. Drain chicken; dredge the breasts in flour, packing flour into crevices and coating well. Deep-fry in hot oil (350° F.) for 10 minutes, or until cooked. Drain in a single layer in a large shallow baking pan.   **YIELD: 8 SERVINGS**

They say that the only book that outsells cookbooks is the Bible, so you can see how serious food is to us. I try not to get serious about food more than three times a day. Or four if I can swing it.

Smothered Chicken

So tender the chicken just falls off the bone ... Serve with biscuits, potatoes, or cooked rice.

1   2½- to 3-pound broiler-fryer, cut up
½   cup plus 2 tablespoons self-rising flour
1   teaspoon salt
½   teaspoon pepper, plus some for gravy
½   cup vegetable oil
1   cup half-and-half
1   cup milk

Rinse chicken pieces and pat dry with paper towels. Combine ½ cup flour, ½ teaspoon salt, and ½ teaspoon pepper, and dredge chicken well in flour mixture. Heat oil in a large heavy skillet over medium-high heat; add chicken and brown well on both sides. Turn chicken skin side up, cover, reduce heat, and simmer 15 minutes. Remove chicken, reserving ¼ cup drippings in skillet.

Combine remaining 2 tablespoons flour, half-and-half, milk, remaining ½ teaspoon salt, and pepper to taste; stir until smooth. Stir into skillet and cook over medium heat until thickened, stirring constantly. Add chicken, turning to coat with gravy; cover and simmer 15 minutes.   **YIELD: 4 TO 6 SERVINGS**

Chicken and Dumplings

These dumplings are light and fluffy. I am amazed at what passes for dumplings these days, so heavy and thick you'd be better off playing baseball with them than eating them.

If you want your sauce to be thicker, like gravy, stir 2 tablespoons flour into ¼ cup milk until smooth, then stir into the simmering broth and stir until thickened.

1 2½- to 3-pound broiler-fryer, cut up, skin removed
6 cups water
1 tablespoon salt
1 teaspoon pepper
1 cup milk
2 tablespoons margarine
⅓ cup shortening
2 cups sifted self-rising flour
½ cup water

Place chicken in a heavy 2½-quart saucepan. Add 6 cups water, and stir in salt and pepper. Bring to a boil, cover, reduce heat, and simmer 45 minutes to 1 hour, or until very tender. Remove chicken from broth; let cool. Remove chicken from bones and dice. Add milk and margarine to broth; bring to a simmer.

Cut shortening into flour using a pastry blender until mixture resembles coarse meal. Add ½ cup water and stir with a fork just until dough leaves side of bowl. For rolled dumplings, roll out dough to ⅛-inch thickness on a lightly floured surface; cut into 4- × ½-inch strips or 2-inch squares. For drop dumplings, pat dough to ½-inch thickness on a lightly floured surface; pinch off dough in 1½-inch pieces. Gradually drop dumplings, one at a time, into boiling broth mixture. Cover, reduce heat, and boil gently for 15 minutes, or until dumplings are cooked. Stir occasionally to prevent sticking. Stir in chicken and heat through. **YIELD: 6 TO 8 SERVINGS**

FANNIE
FLAGG'S
ORIGINAL
WHISTLE STOP
CAFE
COOKBOOK
•
24

I am crazy about firemen. They are just the best. I never met a fireman I didn't like. As a matter of fact, I dated a fireman once. I mean that literally; we just had one date. I decided to make dinner for him and served him chicken and dumplings. But I think I must have forgotten something. I think it was the chicken.

TODAY'S SPECIALS:

CHICKEN 'N' DUMPLINGS

ROAST PORK and APPLESAUCE

COUNTRY FRIED STEAK

POSSUM and SWEET POTATOES

WIENERS and KRAUT with GREEN TOMATO RELISH

TRY OUR: MISSISSIPPI MUD CAKE !

Chicken Pot Pie

Make a lot of these and freeze them for nights when you don't feel like cooking . . . I wonder—can you freeze 365 chicken pot pies?

FILLING

1	2½- to 3-pound broiler-fryer, cut up and skin removed
1	tablespoon salt
1	teaspoon pepper
1	16-ounce bag frozen mixed vegetables, cooked and drained
1	2-ounce jar diced pimiento, drained
⅓	cup self-rising flour
½	cup half-and-half, milk, or water

Melted margarine

PASTRY

2	cups all-purpose flour
1	teaspoon salt
⅔	cup shortening
5	to 6 tablespoons cold water

First make the pastry: Combine flour and salt; cut in shortening with a pastry blender until crumbly. Sprinkle cold water over mixture, 1 tablespoon at a time, tossing with a fork until mixture is dampened. Turn out onto a piece of wax paper and press into a disk. Wrap well and refrigerate.

Place chicken in a heavy medium saucepan, add water to barely cover, and stir in salt and pepper. Bring to a boil, cover, reduce heat, and simmer 45 minutes to 1 hour, or until very tender.

FANNIE
FLAGG'S
ORIGINAL
WHISTLE STOP
CAFE
COOKBOOK
•
26

Remove chicken from broth; let cool. Remove chicken from bones and cut up. Measure out and reserve 4 cups broth; reserve any remaining broth for other uses.

Add chicken, vegetables, and pimiento to broth in saucepan. Combine flour and half-and-half, mixing until smooth. Stir into broth mixture. Cook until thickened, stirring constantly.

Preheat oven to 350° F. Working with half of pastry at a time, roll out on a floured surface into a rectangle ¼ inch thick; cut into ½-inch strips. Arrange half of strips ⅛ inch apart in bottom and up sides of a greased 12- × 8- × 2-inch baking dish, cutting and piecing to fit. Spoon chicken mixture into baking dish. Arrange remaining pastry strips on top, spacing ⅛ inch apart. Brush lightly with melted margarine; bake for 1 hour or until top pastry is golden brown.   **YIELD: 6 TO 8 SERVINGS**

One day as I walked into a fine cafe in Alabama called Jewelyns, I noticed they had a box by the door and they were having a drawing. The sign said WIN A FREE TRIP FOR TWO TO THE CARIBBEAN . . . *OR TWO FREE MEALS AT JEWELYNS.* Most people hoped they would win the two free meals.

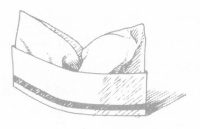

Barbecue Chicken

6 chicken breast quarters, skin removed
Salt
Pepper
⅓ cup margarine, melted (optional)
3 cups Aunt Bess's Barbecue Sauce (page 70),
   heated

Preheat oven to 350° F. Arrange chicken breast quarters in a greased 13- × 9- × 2-inch baking pan. Sprinkle with salt and pepper and brush with margarine, if desired. Cover tightly with aluminum foil; bake 1¼ to 1½ hours, or until tender. Remove foil; pour off drippings. Pour hot barbecue sauce over chicken to serve.   **YIELD: 6 SERVINGS**

I think one of the reasons that Southerners love to eat and why we serve such big portions is that the Depression hit the South especially hard. People really did go hungry and a great many almost starved to death. That fear of not having enough to eat was passed down from your grandparents and parents. I know my mother, who had lived through the Depression and experienced hunger, always kept her pantry stocked full of food. It was unheard of *not* to finish everything on your plate. When Scarlett said, "I'll never go hungry again," she wasn't kidding.

FANNIE
FLAGG'S
ORIGINAL
WHISTLESTOP
CAFE
COOKBOOK
•
28

Baked Turkey With Traditional Cornbread Dressing

Southerners don't care what the bird looks like at the table: For example, my parents' generation and the one before never stuffed a turkey to plump it. They just wanted to make sure there was enough juice to soak up cornbread and biscuit crumbs to make good dressing, with enough small pieces that melt off the bone to stir into the gravy. And some folks cook the whole bird upside down, so the fattier juices will seep down from the dark meat to the white and make the breast more tender. That used to be done before Butterballs and modern-raised turkeys came on the market.

When you wrap the bird in foil, you steam the meat instead of roasting it, so you get a very moist turkey without the basting.

  1 10- to 12-pound turkey, thawed if frozen
Salt
½ cup margarine, melted

Preheat oven to 375° F. Remove giblets and neck from cavity; wash turkey and pat dry with paper towels. Sprinkle inside and outside with salt. Place turkey on 2 large pieces of heavy-duty aluminum foil, crossed at the center. Brush turkey all over with melted margarine. Wrap foil around turkey, blousing foil so it does not stick to turkey during cooking, and sealing tightly. Place in a large roasting pan and bake for 3½ to 4½ hours, or until tender. Remove from oven and carefully loosen foil at one end of roasting pan; pour off drippings into a pan. Combine drippings with enough water to make 2 cups broth; reserve for dressing. Let turkey cool 30 minutes in foil. Remove from foil; remove skin and carve. Serve with cornbread dressing.

YIELD: 12 TO 14 SERVINGS

CORNBREAD DRESSING

6	cups cornbread crumbs
2	cups biscuit crumbs
½	teaspoon salt
1	teaspoon pepper
1½	tablespoons rubbed sage
2	cups chopped celery
1½	cups finely chopped onion
½	cup butter or margarine
⅓	cup water
2	cups reserved broth
½	cup vegetable oil
3	eggs, lightly beaten

Combine first 5 ingredients in a large bowl. Set aside. Combine celery, onion, butter, and water in a medium saucepan; bring to a boil over medium heat. Remove from heat and add to cornbread mixture; stir in broth, oil, and eggs, mixing well. Pour into a greased shallow 2½-quart baking dish and bake, uncovered, at 375° F. for 45 minutes, or until set and golden brown.

YIELD: 12 TO 14 SERVINGS

FANNIE
FLAGG'S
ORIGINAL
WHISTLE STOP
CAFE
COOKBOOK
•
30

Beef Dishes

Oven Roast

Cooking until "very tender" to us means "fall-apart tender."

1	3- to 4-pound boneless rump or eye-of-round roast
1½	tablespoons Worcestershire sauce
½	tablespoon soy sauce
1	teaspoon garlic powder
1	teaspoon seasoned salt
1	teaspoon pepper
	Water
¼	cup self-rising flour

Preheat oven to 325° F. Rub roast with Worcestershire sauce and soy sauce; rub next 3 ingredients into meat. Wrap roast tightly in a double thickness of aluminum foil or in heavy-duty aluminum foil and place in a roasting pan. Bake for 3 to 3½ hours, or until meat is very tender. Carefully unwrap roast, pouring drippings into baking dish. Place roast on a serving platter; keep warm.

Measure drippings; add water to make 3 cups. Pour into a saucepan, add flour, and whisk until smooth. Cook over medium heat until thick and smooth, whisking constantly. Serve with the roast and mashed or boiled new potatoes. **YIELD: 6 TO 8 SERVINGS**

NOTE: For thicker gravy, use ⅓ cup self-rising flour.

Pot Roast

This is without a doubt the best pot roast I have ever

FANNIE
FLAGG'S
ORIGINAL
WHISTLESTOP
CAFE
COOKBOOK
•
32

eaten; it is tender, rich, filling, and satisfying and just *so* good.

1 3-pound chuck or rump roast
1 teaspoon garlic powder
1 teaspoon seasoned salt
1 teaspoon pepper
3 tablespoons vegetable oil
2 cups water, plus some for gravy
1 large onion, peeled and cut into wedges
5 carrots, peeled and cut into 2-inch lengths
3 large or 4 medium russet potatoes, peeled and quartered
½ cup self-rising flour
Salt and pepper to taste

Rub seasonings into meat. Brown roast in oil over medium-high heat in a large, heavy dutch oven. Pour 2 cups water around meat; arrange onion wedges on top of meat. Cover tightly, reduce heat, and simmer 1½ to 2 hours, or until meat is very tender. Add carrots and potatoes to dutch oven, cover tightly, and simmer 30 minutes, or until vegetables are tender.

Remove from heat; transfer roast and vegetables to a serving platter, and keep warm. Measure drippings and add water to make 3 cups. Pour into dutch oven, add flour, and whisk until smooth. Cook over medium heat until mixture is thickened, whisking constantly. Season to taste with salt and pepper. Serve with roast, vegetables, and biscuits. **YIELD: 6 TO 8 SERVINGS**

My Aunt Bess had a sign on her door that said WE OPEN AT SUNRISE AND DON'T CLOSE UNTIL THE LAST DOG IS HUNG. As a child I always wondered what that meant. I guess it said she would never close as long as she had a customer, until everybody went home, and she didn't.

Beef Tips and Rice

3	pounds lean sirloin tip roast
⅓	cup plus 3 tablespoons all-purpose flour
¼	cup plus 1 tablespoon vegetable oil
1	large onion, peeled and chopped
1	green pepper, cored, seeded, and chopped
4⅓	cups water
¼	cup Worcestershire sauce
¼	cup soy sauce
1	teaspoon garlic powder
1	teaspoon seasoned salt
½	to 1 teaspoon pepper

Trim fat from roast, and cut into 1½-inch cubes. Toss with ⅓ cup flour. Set aside.

Heat 2 tablespoons oil in a dutch oven; add onion and green pepper and sauté until tender. Remove and set aside. Add remaining 3 tablespoons oil to dutch oven and heat over medium-high heat. Add beef cubes; brown well. Return vegetables to pot. Add 4 cups water and next 5 ingredients. Bring to a boil, cover partially, reduce heat, and simmer 1 hour.

Combine remaining 3 tablespoons flour with ⅓ cup water; stir well. Stir into beef mixture and cook until thickened. Serve over hot cooked rice. **YIELD: 6 TO 8 SERVINGS**

I am not a political person. But if I had to propose a political platform, I suppose I would ask people to please stop concentrating so hard on all our differences and instead to celebrate all the wonderful and loving ways we are all alike.

FANNIE
FLAGG'S
ORIGINAL
WHISTLE STOP
CAFE
COOKBOOK
•
34

Country-Fried Steak

¾ cup all-purpose flour
½ teaspoon salt
½ teaspoon pepper
4 5-ounce beef cube steaks
¼ cup plus 1 tablespoon vegetable oil
1 cup chopped onion
1 cup water
1 cup milk

Combine first 3 ingredients; measure out and reserve ¼ cup flour mixture. Place remaining ½ cup flour mixture in a shallow dish. Pound steaks to ¼-inch thickness; dredge in flour mixture, coating well on both sides and pressing flour into meat. Heat 3 tablespoons oil in a large, heavy skillet over medium-high heat. Dredge steaks again in any remaining flour mixture and fry until browned on both sides, adding 1 or 2 tablespoons additional oil to skillet if needed. Remove steaks and set aside.

Add onion to skillet, and sauté until lightly browned. Add water, stirring to loosen clinging particles. Return steaks to skillet; cover and simmer 30 minutes, or until tender. Remove steaks, reserving drippings in skillet. Add reserved ¼ cup flour mixture to skillet, stirring until smooth. Cook until lightly browned, stirring constantly. Stir in milk with a wire whisk. Cook, stirring constantly, until thickened. Return steaks to skillet, turning to coat with sauce; simmer until hot.   **YIELD: 4 SERVINGS**

Hamburger Steak with Onions and Gravy

This recipe yields a lot of gravy; naturally it is served with rice and biscuits for sopping.

> 1⅓ pounds ground chuck
> ¾ cup finely chopped onion
> 1 egg
> 1 tablespoon Worcestershire sauce
> 1½ teaspoons seasoned salt
> ¾ teaspoon pepper
> ½ teaspoon garlic powder
> ⅓ cup plus ¼ cup self-rising flour
> 3 tablespoons vegetable oil
> 2 medium onions, peeled and thinly sliced
> 2 cups water
> ½ teaspoon salt

Combine first 4 ingredients with 1 teaspoon seasoned salt, ½ teaspoon pepper, and the garlic powder, mixing well; shape into 4- to 4½-inch patties. Dredge well in ⅓ cup flour. Heat oil in a large heavy skillet over medium-high heat, add patties, and cook until well browned on both sides. Remove from skillet and set aside. Add sliced onion to skillet; reduce heat to medium, and sauté until onion is browned.

Combine water, ¼ cup flour, ½ teaspoon seasoned salt, salt, and ¼ teaspoon pepper; stir until smooth. Stir into skillet and cook, stirring constantly, until thickened. Return steaks to skillet, turning to coat with sauce. Cover, reduce heat, and simmer 15 minutes. **YIELD: 4 SERVINGS**

A good short-order cook is worth her/his weight in gold. They have nerves of steel, and work best under pressure. Watch a short-order cook in any cafe at the breakfast rush

FANNIE
FLAGG'S
ORIGINAL
WHISTLE STOP
CAFE
COOKBOOK
•
36

or the lunch hour. They are a thing of beauty: frying, cutting, buttering, slicing, toasting, grilling, flipping, and never missing a beat. I'll tell you if I were ever in a crisis, and I could have anyone at all with me, I'd take a good short-order cook any time.

Meatloaf

Meatloaf and mashed potatoes . . . is there a better no-nonsense, rock solid American meal? It always makes me feel better.

1¼	cups finely crumbled biscuits or fresh breadcrumbs
1	cup finely chopped onion
1	cup finely chopped green pepper
¼	cup plus 2 tablespoons uncooked regular oats
¼	cup plus 2 tablespoons finely chopped seeded tomatoes
1	teaspoon seasoned salt
½	teaspoon pepper
1	teaspoon rubbed sage
½	teaspoon garlic powder
¼	cup plus 2 tablespoons milk
¼	cup plus 2 tablespoons commercial tomato sauce
2	eggs, beaten
2	pounds ground chuck

Preheat oven to 375° F. Combine first 9 ingredients in a large bowl and mix well. Stir in milk, tomato sauce, and eggs; mix in beef until well blended. Shape into a 10- × 5-inch loaf and place on a broiler rack set in a larger pan. Bake for 1 hour to 1 hour 20 minutes, or until done. **YIELD: 8 TO 10 SERVINGS**

Waitresses

Waitresses are the unsung heroines of the world: They all deserve a medal and certainly a bigger tip.

Was there ever a group of people who worked harder for less pay than the waitresses? They show up day after day, rain or shine, to serve you with a smile. Most have been working an hour setting up before you even get in the door, and still they smile. Most of these gals are raising kids alone, go home after a hard day to cook and clean and fix dinner for their own family, one they can barely afford to feed and clothe, but they smile. Husband may be a drunk or gone, oldest kid may be in jail, youngest kid may need glasses, but you would never know it by the smile. "Hi hon, what are you gonna have today?" For sheer physical endurance, running on their feet in the cafe's marathon, carrying heavy trays all day . . . the spoiled prima donna football and basketball players who rake in millions to play during one season would be hard-pressed to keep up with them. And unlike those guys, these gals work well past their prime. Women who are in their sixties and seventies are still out there slinging hash with no fancy retirement plan or bonuses; they just go until they drop. They may hurt, their feet may be killing them, or they may be worried to death over something, but they still make you feel welcome, will always steer you towards what's good today, or save a piece of the pie they know you like. I can't say enough about waitresses. I have known so many, and I thank you all for your service throughout the years. So whether your waitress is called Thelma, Earline, Neva Jean, or Dot, don't forget that tip. They'll appreciate it.

FANNIE
FLAGG'S
ORIGINAL
WHISTLE STOP
CAFE
COOKBOOK
•
38

Stuffed Peppers

6 to 8 large green peppers
Salt
Pepper
¾ pound ground beef
1 medium onion, peeled and chopped
1½ cups cooked rice
1 14½-ounce can stewed tomatoes, well drained
1 egg, beaten
½ teaspoon salt
¼ teaspoon pepper
Fine dry breadcrumbs or grated Cheddar cheese

Slice off tops of green peppers; scrape out membranes and seeds. Cook peppers in boiling salted water to cover for 3 to 5 minutes. Drain well and rinse under cold water to stop cooking. Pat dry inside and out with dry towels; sprinkle insides with salt and pepper.

Preheat oven to 350° F. Cook ground beef and onion in a skillet until browned, stirring to crumble meat. Drain in a colander. Transfer to a bowl and stir in next 5 ingredients. Stuff pepper cases with mixture and place in a baking dish. Sprinkle tops with breadcrumbs or cheese; bake for 25 minutes.

YIELD: 6 TO 8 SERVINGS

A cafe doesn't always have to be in a small town or even be called a cafe—it's the spirit of the place that counts. People who live in cities still love to go back to the same familiar places, places where people know you. And when they smile at you and ask you how you are, they really want to know.

FANNIE
FLAGG'S
ORIGINAL
WHISTLESTOP
CAFE
COOKBOOK
•
40

Liver and Onions

I always order liver at cafes ... they really can cook it right and you can be sure it is always fresh ... freshness is the secret to good liver dishes.

 1 pound calf or beef liver
Salt
Pepper
All-purpose flour
¼ cup plus 2 tablespoons butter or margarine
 2 large onions, peeled and thinly sliced
 2 tablespoons all-purpose flour
¾ cup plus 2 tablespoons beef broth
¾ cup sour cream (optional)

Sprinkle liver with salt and pepper and dredge well in flour. Cook in 2 tablespoons melted butter in a large skillet until liver loses its pink color and is lightly browned. Remove from skillet and set aside.

Melt ¼ cup butter in skillet over medium heat. Add onions and sauté until tender and lightly browned. Sprinkle flour over onions, stir well, and cook 1 minute, stirring constantly. Add beef broth; cook, stirring constantly, until thickened and bubbly. Add liver to sauce; cover and simmer 10 minutes. Remove from heat; transfer liver to a serving platter. Stir sour cream into skillet and pour sauce over liver. Serve with hot buttered noodles or rice. **YIELD: 4 SERVINGS**

Pork Dishes

FANNIE
FLAGG'S
ORIGINAL
WHISTLE STOP
CAFE
COOKBOOK

•

42

Mr. Pig

$\mathcal{T}$hank you, Mr. Pig . . . there's nothing about pork I don't like. What is now being referred to as the "other white meat" has always been plain ole pork to me, and I have always loved it. But I found out the hard way that some people don't have the same affection that Southerners have for Mr. Pig. While we were filming *Fried Green Tomatoes*, we were out scouting locations for grocery stores when I wandered into a Piggly Wiggly with a Yankee member of our crew. I stopped by the meat section, noticing something you don't often see in Los Angeles. They had pig's feet, pig ears, pig tails, pig snouts, all neatly wrapped in cellophane ready to be sold. My companion obviously had never seen such a thing, and was frozen in horror. Not knowing her terror of simple little pig parts, I proceeded to pick up a pair of ears and a snout and turned to her and jokingly made a snorting sound. I thought this was hilarious. She, on the other hand, apparently did not. I know this because she ran through Piggly Wiggly screaming like a crazy person, and we haven't seen her since.

How to Bake a Fresh Ham or Half Ham

They say you are what you eat, so I serve this to myself and all my actor friends.

Using a sharp knife, cut off the skin and most of the fat on a 10- to 12-pound pork leg (fresh ham) or a 5- to 7-pound pork leg half, leaving just a thin layer of fat on top side. Score this layer of fat into a diamond design, place in a shallow baking pan, and insert a meat thermometer, making sure it does not touch fat or bone. Cover securely with aluminum foil.

   Bake at 350° F. for 1 hour; reduce oven temperature to 300° F. and continue baking 1 to 3 additional hours, or until meat thermometer registers 160° F. (18 to 20 minutes per pound for whole leg and 25 to 30 minutes per pound for half leg). About 30 minutes before ham is done, remove from oven, uncover, and stud with cloves. Combine ½ cup firmly packed brown sugar and ¼ cup cola; spread over top of ham. Continue baking, uncovered, until ham is done. Decorate with maraschino cherry halves and pineapple slices, if desired. **YIELD: 2 TO 3 SERVINGS PER POUND**

NOTE: Put Coca Cola or Dr. Pepper in a frying pan and heat up leftover ham—it really picks up the flavor. You'll be surprised how good it tastes.

FANNIE
FLAGG'S
ORIGINAL
WHISTLE STOP
CAFE
COOKBOOK
•
44

Country Ham with Red-Eye Gravy

You will not end up with a lot of gravy, but this is sweet, truly a case where a little goes a long, long way.

    4 to 6 ¼-inch-thick slices cooked country ham
    1 cup strong coffee
    1 tablespoon white or brown sugar

Cut off and discard rind from ham. Trim off and reserve excess fat, leaving a small amount of fat around edge. Cut gashes in fat to keep ham from curling. Place trimmed fat pieces in a large heavy skillet and heat over medium-low heat. Add ham slices and cook until browned, turning several times. Place on a platter and keep warm in a 200° F. oven.

Add coffee and sugar to skillet and bring to a boil over medium heat, stirring to loosen clinging particles. Reduce heat and simmer 4 to 5 minutes, or until slightly thickened, stirring frequently. Remove and discard pieces of fat; spoon gravy over ham.   **YIELD: 4 TO 6 SERVINGS**

Baked Ham
and Pineapple Rings

1   3-inch-thick center-cut smoked ham slice
1   20-ounce can sliced pineapple in syrup, undrained
1   cup cider vinegar
1   cup firmly packed light brown sugar
1   tablespoon Worcestershire sauce
½   teaspoon ground ginger

Trim fat from ham. Place ham in a baking dish just large enough to hold it. Drain pineapple, reserving juice; add remaining ingredients to juice and mix well. Spoon over ham. Cover and refrigerate 3 to 4 hours or overnight. Uncover and bake at 300° F. for 2 hours, basting occasionally. Arrange pineapple slices over ham; baste with sauce and bake 1 additional hour, basting frequently.   **YIELD: 6 TO 8 SERVINGS**

Some cafes have decided on theme decoration. One cafe in Georgia has a . . . well, pig decor motif. You haven't lived until you've eaten in a room full of a thousand pigs. Aunt Bess's idea of decoration was a railroad calendar and a deer's head with Christmas balls hanging on it. Her chances of being featured in Gourmet were pretty slim but her customers ate it up, you might say.

FANNIE
FLAGG'S
ORIGINAL
WHISTLESTOP
CAFE
COOKBOOK
•
46

Smothered Pork Chops

These just fall off the bone and melt in the mouth.

　1　tablespoon brown sugar
　½　teaspoon salt
　¼　teaspoon pepper
　6　¾-inch-thick pork chops
All-purpose flour
Hot bacon drippings
　1　medium onion, peeled and sliced
　1　medium green pepper, cored, seeded, and sliced
　1　lemon, sliced and seeded
Water

　　Combine sugar, salt, and pepper; rub mixture onto both sides of pork chops. Coat chops well with flour. Fry in ¼ inch of hot bacon drippings in a large heavy skillet until browned on both sides; remove from skillet and set aside. Add onion and green pepper; sauté until just tender. Return chops to skillet. Add lemon slices and water to come ½ inch up sides of pan. Cover and simmer over low heat 1 to 1½ hours, or until very tender, adding additional water if necessary.　**YIELD: 6 SERVINGS**

　　The town cafe serves many purposes, but there is no group more grateful to the cafe than the retired men, unless it is the wives of retired men. One told me that if her husband did not have the cafe to go to every day and get him out from under her feet for a few hours she would never get her housework done at all.

Pork Chops with Apples and Sweet Potatoes

6 ¾-inch pork chops
All-purpose flour
¼ cup bacon drippings
1 medium onion, peeled and chopped
1 cup apple juice
1 tablespoon Worcestershire sauce
4 medium apples, peeled and cut into ½-inch slices
4 medium sweet potatoes, peeled and cut into
    ½-inch slices
Salt and pepper to taste

Coat pork chops with flour; brown on both sides in hot bacon drippings. Place pork chops in a casserole just large enough to hold them in a single layer. Add onion to skillet; sauté until tender. Add apple juice and Worcestershire sauce and bring to a boil, stirring to loosen clinging particles. Remove from heat.

Preheat oven to 350° F. Arrange alternate layers of apples and sweet potatoes on top of chops, sprinkling with salt and pepper as you layer. Pour apple juice mixture over everything, cover tightly, and bake for 1½ hours. **YIELD: 6 SERVINGS**

FANNIE
FLAGG'S
ORIGINAL
WHISTLESTOP
CAFE
COOKBOOK
•
48

Possum and Veal Dishes

FANNIE
FLAGG'S
ORIGINAL
WHISTLESTOP
CAFE
COOKBOOK
•
50

Roast Possum

For Yankees or anyone else who cannot locate possum, substitute pork.

½   cup herb stuffing mix
¼   cup golden raisins
¼   cup chopped pecans
2   tablespoons chopped onion
2   tablespoons chopped celery
2   tablespoons minced fresh parsley
½   teaspoon rubbed sage
½   teaspoon dried Italian seasoning
1   plump possum; or two 1-pound pork tenderloins
1   lemon, cut in half
Salt
Pepper
½   cup apricot jam
2   tablespoons bourbon

Preheat oven to 375° F. Combine first 8 ingredients in a bowl; mix well. Rub tenderloins with cut halves of lemon and sprinkle with salt and pepper. Make a lengthwise slit down center of each tenderloin, cutting to within ½ inch of bottom; open tenderloins. Fill centers with stuffing, pull outer edges of each tenderloin together over stuffing, and tie each tenderloin with kitchen string. Place on a rack in a shallow baking pan; bake for 30 to 40 minutes, or until done. Transfer to a serving dish. Combine jam and bourbon and spoon over meat.   YIELD: 8 SERVINGS

Veal Parmigiana

2 pounds veal cutlets, cut into serving-size pieces
2 eggs, beaten
¼ teaspoon garlic powder
¼ teaspoon salt
¾ teaspoon pepper
Fine dry breadcrumbs
⅓ cup vegetable oil
1 15-ounce can tomato sauce
1 8-ounce can tomato sauce
2 tablespoons brown sugar
1½ teaspoons dried oregano leaves
¼ cup grated Parmesan cheese
1 8-ounce package sliced mozzarella cheese

Pound veal cutlets, if necessary, to ⅛-inch thickness. Combine eggs and next 2 ingredients, and ¼ teaspoon of pepper in a bowl; beat well with a wire whisk. Add cutlets, turning to coat with egg mixture; cover and let stand 15 minutes. Drain and dredge well with breadcrumbs. Cook cutlets in hot oil until browned on each side. Place in a lightly greased 13- × 9- × 2-inch baking dish.

Preheat oven to 350° F. Combine tomato sauce, brown sugar, oregano, and ½ teaspoon pepper in a saucepan. Bring to a boil, stirring frequently. Pour sauce over veal and sprinkle with Parmesan cheese. Cover and bake for 30 minutes. Uncover and arrange mozzarella cheese slices on top of cutlets; bake 5 to 10 additional minutes. **YIELD: 6 SERVINGS**

Whenever there is a dispute of any kind going on, whether it is between people, organizations or countries, you often hear it said that "the parties have come to the table" for discussions. I think we should go a step further and have a nice hot meal on the table for them to enjoy. I'll bet it would help everyone get to the heart of the matter faster.

FANNIE
FLAGG'S
ORIGINAL
WHISTLESTOP
CAFE
COOKBOOK
•
52

Fish

ong before there were official recreation centers or senior citizens centers, the cafe served as both. If you wanted a good game of cards or checkers you went on down to the cafe. Most cafes had some sort of bench out front where old men sat all day and watched the world go by. A fish fry was usually held out in back of the cafe and was usually to raise money for a church or to provide the backdrop for a local politician's speech. They say more catfish got politicians elected in Alabama than political issues.

Creatures That Swim

I must be honest with you. I do not care very much for fish. I only like it if it tastes like chicken, in which case I am better off just ordering the chicken in the first place. Believe it or not, that bit of wisdom took me years to come by. I spent years of my life ordering fish because I know how good it is supposed to be for you, but when some poor, unsuspecting waitress would bring it to the table, I would take a bite, make a face, and complain to anyone who would listen, *"This stuff tastes just like fish!"* and push it away.

This sort of logic is why I am a writer. You don't want me around when there is serious problem-solving involved. I did not even come by this wisdom alone:

Scene: Cafe at lunch, Fannie comes in, sits down, waitress comes over . . .

Waitress: "Hi, hon, what are you going to have today?"

Fannie: "What kind of fresh fish do you have?"

Waitress: "Flounder, catfish, speckled trout, bass, sole . . ."

Fannie: "Which one tastes less like fish?"

Waitress: "The chicken."

Fannie: "Oh, right, I'll have the chicken."

My daddy, unlike myself, loved fish, and he often told us that if anything ever happened to him, to go ahead and throw him off the end of the pier he had fished from for so many years. Daddy said he had enjoyed so many fine fish in his day that they should have a crack at him in return.

FANNIE
FLAGG'S
ORIGINAL
WHISTLE STOP
CAFE
COOKBOOK

•

54

Fried Catfish

Serve with slaw and hushpuppies and you have a meal fit for a king or queen.

       6   medium catfish, cleaned and dressed
       ½   teaspoon salt
       ¼   teaspoon pepper
           Hot sauce (optional)
       1   cup self-rising flour
       1   cup self-rising cornmeal
       ¼   cup bacon drippings or shortening

Sprinkle catfish on both sides with salt and pepper; if desired, douse with hot sauce. Let stand at room temperature 10 minutes. Combine flour and cornmeal and dredge catfish in mixture. Fry in hot bacon drippings about 8 to 10 minutes, turning once, or until golden brown on both sides.   **YIELD: 6 SERVINGS**

Most of my Aunt Bess's customers were railroad men and were in the cafe by 5:00 A.M. for their breakfast. They ate their lunch and dinner there. Most of these sweet old guys had been in World War One and had never married. They just drifted from town to town. I was told years later that on their railroad insurance burial policies, where it said "next of kin," most of them wrote in my Aunt Bess's name. She always made sure they had a decent burial.

FANNIE
FLAGG'S
ORIGINAL
WHISTLE STOP
CAFE
COOKBOOK
•
56

Salmon Croquettes

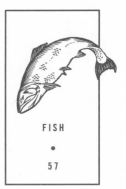
1   15½-ounce can pink salmon, drained
1   medium onion, peeled and finely chopped
3   tablespoons margarine, melted
¾   cup finely crushed saltines
2   tablespoons self-rising flour, plus some for
    coating
¼   teaspoon pepper
1   egg, beaten
3   tablespoons milk
1   tablespoon lemon juice
Vegetable oil

Remove skin and bones from salmon; flake salmon with a
fork. Sauté onion in margarine until tender, remove from heat,
and stir in salmon and everything else but the oil. Form into
1- **x** 1- **x** 2½-inch croquettes or small balls; coat with additional
flour, and deep-fry in hot oil (375° F.) until golden brown. Drain.
YIELD: 4 TO 6 SERVINGS

*"By now, the name of the
cafe was written on the
walls of hundreds of
boxcars, from Seattle to
Florida. Splinter Belly
Jones said he had seen it
as far away as Canada.
    Things were
especially bad that year,
and at night the woods
all around Whistle Stop
twinkled from the fires
at the hobo camps, and
there wasn't a single
man there that Idgie
and Ruth had not fed at
one time or another."*

Trout Amandine

½ cup sliced almonds
¼ cup butter or margarine, melted
6 large trout fillets
Salt and pepper to taste
Dried thyme leaves to taste
Milk
All-purpose flour
½ cup vegetable oil
1 tablespoon minced fresh parsley
Lemon wedges

Sauté almonds in butter in a large heavy skillet until golden brown; do not let butter burn. Transfer to a bowl and set aside. Sprinkle fillets with salt, pepper, and thyme; dip in milk and dredge in flour. Fry fillets in hot oil (360° F.) in skillet over medium heat until golden brown, turning once. Drain on paper towels. Transfer to a serving platter; sprinkle with almonds and parsley and drizzle with any remaining browned butter. Serve with lemon wedges. **YIELD: 6 SERVINGS**

FANNIE
FLAGG'S
ORIGINAL
WHISTLESTOP
CAFE
COOKBOOK
•
58

Down Home Crab Cakes

½ cup mayonnaise
1 egg, beaten
⅓ cup minced green or sweet red pepper
3 tablespoons minced onion
⅓ cup cooked white corn kernels (optional)
1 teaspoon dry mustard
¼ to ½ teaspoon pepper
1 pound fresh lump crabmeat, drained and flaked
About 2 cups fresh breadcrumbs or finely crumbled
biscuits
2 tablespoons butter
2 tablespoons vegetable oil
Tartar sauce

Combine mayonnaise and egg in a large bowl; mix in next 5 ingredients. Stir in crabmeat and 1 to 1¼ cups breadcrumbs, or enough to hold mixture together. Shape into 8 patties. Coat patties with remaining breadcrumbs.

Heat butter and oil in a large heavy skillet; add crab cakes, in batches and fry until lightly browned on both sides. Serve with tartar sauce.   **YIELD: 4 SERVINGS**

When Aunt Bess started the cafe there was no such thing as a pension plan, but all of the cooks who worked for her had jobs for life and their children somehow all managed to go to college. Bess never married but she had plenty of children she loved and who loved her as much as if she were family. She used to say, "Honey, they may put Miss on my tombstone, but, believe me, I haven't missed a thing."

Fried Oysters

1   12-ounce container fresh select oysters, drained
1   egg, beaten
1   tablespoon water
2   teaspoons hot sauce
1½ cups very finely crushed saltine cracker crumbs
⅓   cup white cornmeal
¼   to ½ teaspoon salt
Vegetable oil

Pat oysters dry with paper towels. Combine egg, water, and hot sauce; mix well. Combine cracker crumbs, cornmeal, and salt. Dip oysters in egg mixture, and roll individually in cracker crumb mixture. Fry in 2 inches hot oil (375° F.) for 1 to 2 minutes, or until golden brown. Drain on paper towels.

YIELD: 3 SERVINGS

FANNIE
FLAGG'S
ORIGINAL
WHISTLESTOP
CAFE
COOKBOOK
•
60

Scalloped Oysters

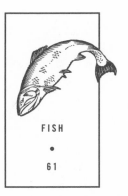

¼ cup minced onion
½ cup butter or margarine, melted
¾ teaspoon celery or seasoned salt
¼ to ½ teaspoon red pepper
1 tablespoon Worcestershire sauce
1 teaspoon lemon juice
2 cups saltine cracker crumbs
1 tablespoon parsley flakes
2 12-ounce containers fresh standard oysters
2 eggs, beaten
1 cup half-and-half

Sauté onion in butter until tender. Remove from heat and stir in next 4 ingredients. Combine cracker crumbs and parsley flakes. Preheat oven to 350° F. Drain oysters, reserving ⅓ cup liquor. Sprinkle ½ cup cracker crumbs in bottom of a lightly greased 8-inch square baking dish; layer half of oysters and half of remaining cracker crumb mixture. Drizzle with half of butter mixture. Repeat layers. Combine eggs, half-and-half, and reserved oyster liquor; mix well. Pour over oyster layers. Bake for 40 to 45 minutes, or until set. **YIELD: 6 SERVINGS**

It saddens me to think of all the people in this country who have travelled all over the world who have yet to travel to the Southern part of the United States. Unlike the French we would be so happy to see you. And we even speak the same language . . . sort of.

Fried Shrimp

2 pounds fresh unpeeled medium-size shrimp
4 eggs, beaten
⅔ cup mayonnaise
3 tablespoons lemon juice
1 teaspoon garlic powder
1⅓ cups saltine cracker crumbs
1 cup cornflake cereal crumbs
⅓ cup cornmeal
Vegetable oil
Cocktail sauce

Peel and devein shrimp, leaving tails intact. Combine eggs and next 3 ingredients in a large bowl; mix well and stir in shrimp gently. Cover and chill 3 to 4 hours or until time to fry.

Combine cracker crumbs, cereal crumbs, and cornmeal. Remove shrimp from marinade and discard marinade. Dredge shrimp in crumb mixture, pressing to adhere. Deep-fry in hot oil (375° F.) until golden. Drain on paper towels. Serve with cocktail sauce. **YIELD: 4 TO 6 SERVINGS**

FANNIE
FLAGG'S
ORIGINAL
WHISTLE STOP
CAFE
COOKBOOK
•
62

GRAVIES AND SAUCES

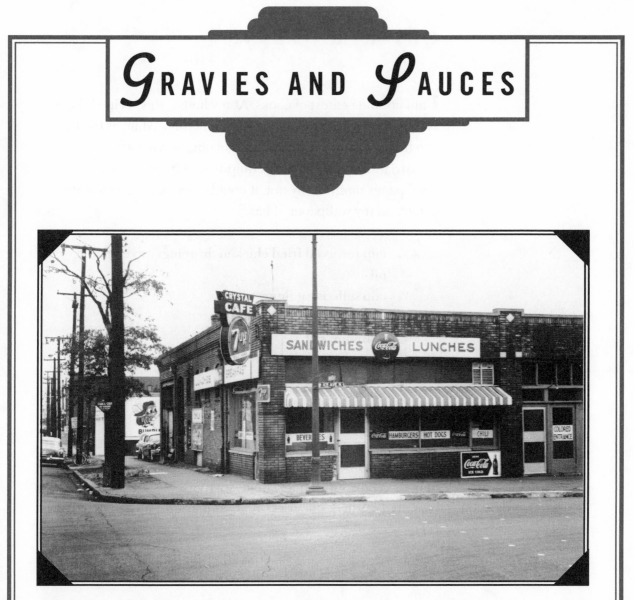

What's Sauce for the Goose is Gravy Down Home

A good gravy is like a good black dress: It can hide a multitude of imperfections. In fact you can put a really good cream gravy over cardboard and it would still make a delicious dinner. I'm sure I've had it a couple of times myself and it was good. Anyway, what you don't know will not hurt you, and a wonderful, warm gravy can transform mystery meat into the best meal you ever had.

Chicken Gravy

I am not the neatest of cooks. At my house, this recipe is known as Completely Mess Up Your Kitchen Gravy. Many is the time I've had to call in a professional cleaning service with industrial strength cleaning equipment. Gravy stains as a wallpaper motif? Why not, it could catch on. . . . As a matter of fact, on my wallpaper, it has.

¼ cup reserved fried chicken drippings or vegetable oil
¼ cup self-rising flour
2 cups milk
½ teaspoon salt
¼ teaspoon pepper

Fry chicken in a cast-iron skillet, then measure out and pour ¼ cup drippings back into the skillet.

Combine drippings and flour in large heavy skillet and cook over medium heat until color is pale brown. Stir in milk, salt, and pepper; cook until thickened, stirring constantly. Serve over biscuits, mashed potatoes, rice, and fried chicken.   **YIELD: 2 CUPS**

FANNIE
FLAGG'S
ORIGINAL
WHISTLESTOP
CAFE
COOKBOOK
•
64

Giblet Gravy

This makes enough for a family turkey dinner, with leftovers for sandwiches the next day, and revives not only the turkey, but your appetite.

- 3 cups chicken or turkey broth
- ¼ cup all-purpose flour
- 1 10¾-ounce can cream of chicken soup, undiluted
- ½ to ¾ cup chopped giblets or pieces of chicken or turkey
- 3 hard-cooked eggs, chopped

Pepper to taste

Mix broth and flour until smooth in a medium saucepan. Stir in remaining ingredients; cook, stirring constantly, until hot and thickened.   **YIELD: ABOUT 5 CUPS**

Southern hospitality is really what it is cracked up to be.
I know of some Yankees who came for just a short visit and
never went back home. A man in Fairhope, Alabama
arrived for an afternoon in June of 1943, just down from
Boston, and he is still sitting on the front porch having iced
tea to this very day.

Southern Cream Gravy

¼ cup bacon or sausage drippings
¼ cup self-rising flour
1 cup milk
1 cup water
½ teaspoon salt
¼ teaspoon pepper

Combine drippings and flour in a large heavy skillet. Cook over medium heat until color is pale brown. Stir in milk, water, salt, and pepper; cook until thickened, stirring constant-ly. **YIELD: 2 CUPS**

FANNIE
FLAGG'S
ORIGINAL
WHISTLE STOP
CAFE
COOKBOOK
•
66

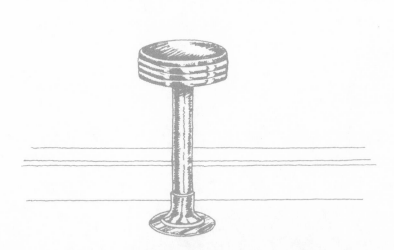

Sausage Gravy

This has a little kick to it, and is my favorite sauce over biscuits—this and a hot cup of coffee makes a meal.

1 pound mild bulk pork sausage
2 tablespoons all-purpose flour
⅔ to 1 cup milk
¼ to ½ teaspoon pepper

Cook sausage in a large heavy skillet until browned, stirring to crumble. Remove from skillet using a slotted spoon, and drain well. Reserve 2 tablespoons drippings in skillet. Add flour to drippings, stirring until smooth. Cook over medium heat, stirring constantly, for 1 minute. Gradually add ⅔ cup milk, stirring constantly until smooth and thickened. Add remaining ⅓ cup milk, if you want gravy thinner. Stir in pepper and sausage; cook until hot, stirring constantly. Serve over split biscuits.

YIELD: 3 TO 4 SERVINGS

Barbecue Blues

*H*ave you ever had the homesick barbecue blues? When I moved to California, I found myself surrounded by health freaks. A person would be hard pressed to find a spot of grease on anything except maybe the undercarriage of a car, so you can well imagine the looks of horror I got from people when I talked about Southern food. On the other hand, I would sit and poke at the dime-sized nouvelle cuisine on my plate, usually tiny, sickly green beans that were raw. Miserable and hungry, I would often stare off into space wistfully and murmur to myself: I'd kill for a good old greasy barbecue right now. After my dinner partners had picked up their plates and moved three seats away, they would proceed to lecture me in loud voices about the dangers of barbecue. Oh, yeah, I thought . . . tell that to my ninety-eight-year-old grandmother.

Everybody in the South loves barbecue and each state thinks theirs is the best. That is typical narrow-mindedness. Of course, I think Alabama has the best barbecue in the South. But then the South has the best barbecue in the world. I have long since stopped ordering barbecue anywhere north of the Mason Dixon line or west of Texas. What passes for barbecue beyond those boundaries would break your heart. It might well break your car window if someone threw it at you, because it's always too thick, too tough. Barbecue should be light and falling off the bone, melt-in-your-mouth tender, and the sauce must be just right, not too sour, not too sweet, and the presentation must be correct.

It is not a simple matter to assemble the perfect barbecue plate. First of all, the cafe has to be authentic, the older and seedier the better. Give me those out-of-the-way joints where the old wooden booths, usually made from knotty pine, have acquired over the years an indescribable hickory smoke smell.

Then there is the plate itself. It must be round, thin, cheap, white, and paper. On the ideal plate you will find sliced sour pickles and plenty of runny coleslaw on the side and if you are lucky a huge glob of day-old baked beans. As for the beverage, madame, the wine, I have found that a Grapico or an orange crush is best. For dessert, a substantial slice of

FANNIE
FLAGG'S
ORIGINAL
WHISTLE STOP
CAFE
COOKBOOK
•
68

lemon ice box pie with a graham cracker crust, and a cup of strong hot coffee. Now that's what I call a barbecue d-i-n-n-e-r!

As for the proper attire, a word to the wise. There is no way to be dainty eating barbecue. After you eat it, they may have to take you outside and hose you down. But it's worth it.

"I'd pay a million dollars for a barbecue like Big George used to make, and a piece of Sipsey's lemon ice box pie. He made the best barbecue.

He cooked it in a big old iron drum, out in the back of the cafe, and you could smell it for miles around, especially on a fall day. I could smell it all the way over to my house. Smokey said he was coming in on the train one time and he smelled it ten miles up the tracks from Whistle Stop. People drove all the way from Birmingham to get it."

Aunt Bess's Barbecue Sauce

You may add a tiny drop of liquid smoke if you like a smokey flavor.

½	cup water
¼	cup cider vinegar
¼	cup butter or margarine
2	tablespoons sugar
2	tablespoons Worcestershire sauce
1	tablespoon prepared mustard
1½	teaspoons salt
½	teaspoon black pepper
¼	teaspoon red pepper
1	thick slice lemon
1	thick slice peeled onion
½	cup catsup

Combine all ingredients except catsup in a heavy medium saucepan; bring to a boil, stirring frequently. Reduce heat and simmer, partially covered, for 20 minutes. Remove from heat; discard lemon and onion slices, and stir in catsup.   **YIELD: 1½ CUPS**

FANNIE
FLAGG'S
ORIGINAL
WHISTLE STOP
CAFE
COOKBOOK
•
70

Alabama Sauce Beautiful
(for chicken and pork)

I love a sweet sauce on meat ... it makes it fun to eat.

1 cup water
¼ cup lemon juice
¼ cup plus 2 tablespoons firmly packed brown
sugar
¼ cup butter or margarine
2 tablespoons cider vinegar
1 tablespoon paprika
2 teaspoons Worcestershire sauce
¾ teaspoon salt
½ teaspoon pepper

Combine all ingredients in a saucepan; bring to a boil, stirring constantly until sugar melts. Boil, uncovered, until reduced to 1⅓ cups.   **YIELD: 1⅓ CUPS**

"It was another ice-cold Alabama afternoon, and the hogs were boiling in the big iron pot out in back of the cafe. The pot was bubbling over the top, full of long-gone hogs that would soon be smothered with Big George's special barbecue sauce."

$\mathcal{S}$IDE $\mathcal{D}$ISHES

$\mathcal{Y}$ou don't have to tell a Southerner to "eat your vegetables." We love them. I know people who have their mothers send them frozen homemade turnip greens to New York.

There's not a Tomato Safe South of the Mason-Dixon Line

When the movie *Fried Green Tomatoes* came out it suddenly seemed that every cafe, restaurant, and cafeteria started serving fried green tomatoes. One night we were in Atlanta and my friend, Dan Martin, took me to an exclusive, decidedly elegant restaurant. The captain, after announcing a long list of exotic entrées, announced that of course no dinner would be complete without their specialty, fried green tomatoes.

Dan whispered to me: "I wish you had a piece of the tomato market, I heard the prices have quadrupled and restaurant buyers are having fistfights trying to get the best green ones." I can't help but feel a little bit guilty, however. I have caused thousands of poor little green tomatoes to go to an early picking. But I couldn't help it. They taste so good. People ask me why I think they are popular in the South. Like most of this food, it really started getting to be a popular dish during the Depression. People would fry up most anything and pretend it was meat or fish, and actually, as it turned out, a pitcher of sweet iced tea and a plate of fried green tomatoes turned out to be a delightfully tasty and light summer supper on nights when it was so hot you didn't feel like having a big heavy meal.

So some hot summer night fix yourself a plate of fried green tomatoes, a pitcher of iced tea, and go out on the screen porch and watch the fireflies and listen to the sounds of the night birds and the crickets instead of the six o'clock news. You'll never regret it.

FANNIE
FLAGG'S
ORIGINAL
WHISTLE STOP
CAFE
COOKBOOK
•
74

Fried Green Tomatoes I

To keep the cooked tomatoes from getting soggy before they are served, stand them up like wheels in the serving dish instead of stacking them.

    ¾   cup self-rising flour
    ¼   cup cornmeal
    ¼   teaspoon salt
    ¼   teaspoon pepper
    ¾   cup milk
    3   to 4 green tomatoes, cut into ¼-inch slices
    Vegetable oil

Combine first 5 ingredients; mix until smooth. Add additional milk to thin, if necessary; batter should resemble pancake batter. Working in batches, dip tomato slices into batter, allowing excess batter to drip back into bowl. Fry in 2 inches hot oil (375° F.) in a large heavy skillet until browned, turning once carefully with tongs. Transfer to a colander to drain.   YIELD: 3 TO 4 SERVINGS

In making the movie Fried Green Tomatoes, some of the best times were when Kathy Bates, who is from Memphis, and knows good food, and I used to sneak off and eat some of that wonderful Georgia cooking.

I had a small part in the film and was unfortunately fitted before the movie started. When it was time to film my scene, the dress had suddenly shrunk several sizes. I think it was the Georgia heat that caused it. That's my story and I'm sticking to it.

FANNIE
FLAGG'S
ORIGINAL
WHISTLESTOP
CAFE
COOKBOOK
•
76

Fried Green Tomatoes II

Don't crowd the skillet when frying green tomatoes. Keep them in a single layer, with plenty of space in between slices. If too many are put in the pan, the oil temperature will be lowered and the food will absorb the grease rather than be seared by it, resulting in soggy tomatoes.

1   egg, beaten
1   cup buttermilk
1   cup self-rising flour
⅓   cup cornmeal
½   teaspoon salt
6   to 8 green tomatoes, cut into ¼-inch slices
Bacon drippings, vegetable oil, or mixture of both

Mix egg and buttermilk in a shallow dish. Mix flour, cornmeal, and salt in a shallow dish. Working in batches, dip tomato slices into egg mixture, allowing excess to drip back into dish. Coat with flour mixture. Fry in hot bacon drippings (375° F.) in a large heavy skillet until browned, turning once with tongs. Transfer to a colander to drain.   **YIELD: 6 SERVINGS**

"The place was jam-packed full of railroad men at lunchtime, so Grady Kilgore went to the kitchen door and hollered in, 'Fix me a mess of them fried green tomatoes and some ice tea, will ya, Sipsey? I'm in a hurry.'"

Fried Green Tomatoes with Milk Gravy

¼ cup bacon drippings
4 green tomatoes, sliced ½-inch thick
2 eggs, beaten
Fine dry breadcrumbs
All-purpose flour
Milk
Salt
Pepper

Heat bacon drippings in a large heavy skillet over medium-high heat. Dip tomatoes in eggs, then coat with breadcrumbs. Fry in bacon drippings until golden brown on both sides, adjusting heat to fry slowly. Transfer tomatoes to a serving platter, using a slotted spatula. Measure drippings remaining in skillet; return to skillet. For each tablespoon drippings, stir in 1 tablespoon flour until smooth. Cook over low heat for 1 minute, stirring constantly. For each tablespoon flour you have used, stir in 1 cup milk, ½ teaspoon salt, and ¼ teaspoon pepper until smooth. Cook until thickened, stirring constantly; pour over tomatoes. **YIELD: 4 TO 6 SERVINGS**

FANNIE
FLAGG'S
ORIGINAL
WHISTLESTOP
CAFE
COOKBOOK
•
78

How to Fix a
Pot of Dried Beans,
such as Great Northern Beans,
Pinto Beans, Large Lima Beans,
Navy Beans, or if You Prefer,
Black-Eyed Peas

I sometimes use about 4 to 5 slices of bacon instead of
salt pork.

> 2 cups dried beans
> 6 cups boiling water
> 1½ ounces salt pork, or a small ham hock
> Water
> 1 teaspoon salt

Pour beans onto a small plate, in batches, and discard tiny
pieces or pebbles or any beans with holes. Place beans in a large
bowl and pour boiling water over them. Let stand 2 hours.

Rinse salt pork; cut an "**x**" in top of cube, cutting to but not
through rind. Combine salt pork, 5 cups water, and 1 teaspoon
salt in a dutch oven. Drain beans and add. Bring to a boil, cover,
reduce heat, and simmer 1½ to 2 hours or until tender, adding
more water if necessary to keep beans barely covered.
YIELD: 4 TO 6 SERVINGS

NOTE: When cooking Great Northern beans, add a clove of garlic,
minced, or ¼ teaspoon garlic powder.

There is a tradition that says that if you eat black-eyed peas
on New Year's Day you will have good luck all year long.
I believe it. I have never missed having black-eyed peas
on that day and I have had the best of luck every year.
Good food and good health and good friends.

Baked Beans

3 strips bacon
1 medium onion, peeled and chopped
3 16-ounce cans pork and beans, undrained
½ cup firmly packed light brown sugar
½ cup catsup
¼ teaspoon pepper

Preheat oven to 350° F. Cook bacon until crisp; remove from skillet and drain on paper towels. Crumble bacon and set aside. Add onion to skillet and sauté until golden. Remove from heat and stir in crumbled bacon and remaining ingredients; mix well. Pour into a greased 1½- to 2-quart baking dish. Bake, uncovered, for 30 to 40 minutes.   **YIELD: 8 TO 10 SERVINGS**

Fresh Beets

1½ pounds fresh small beets (each about 1½ inches in diameter)
2 tablespoons butter or margarine (optional)

Trim beets to within 1 inch of crowns; wash well with a brush, but do not scrub too vigorously and break the skin. Place in a saucepan; cover with warm water. Bring to a boil, cover partially, reduce heat, and simmer 25 to 30 minutes, or until tender. Drain in a colander, then pour cold water over beets and drain. Let cool slightly; trim ends and slip off skins. (If skins do not come off easily with slight pressure, they probably need to cook longer.) Cut into ½-inch slices, and toss with melted butter, if desired.   **YIELD: 4 TO 6 SERVINGS**

FANNIE
FLAGG'S
ORIGINAL
WHISTLESTOP
CAFE
COOKBOOK
•
80

Harvard Beets

　3　tablespoons sugar
　1　tablespoon plus 1 teaspoon cornstarch
　½　teaspoon salt
　½　cup water
　¼　cup cider vinegar
　1　tablespoon butter or margarine
3½　cups sliced cooked fresh or drained canned
　　　beets

Combine first 3 ingredients in a medium saucepan; stir well. Gradually add water and vinegar, stirring until smooth. Add butter; cook over medium heat, stirring constantly until butter melts and mixture is thickened. Add beets and cook until hot, stirring frequently. **YIELD: 4 TO 6 SERVINGS**

When I first moved to New York to try to become an actress, I used to take the train home to Birmingham when I could afford it and as the train passed through Irondale I would see my Aunt Bess and the cook and whatever customers happened to be there at the time standing outside in front of the cafe, waving. It was always at that moment, I knew I was really home.

Broccoli Casserole

1   1½-pound bunch broccoli
1   10¾-ounce can cream of mushroom soup, undiluted
½   cup milk
1   cup crushed saltines
1½   cups (6 ounces) shredded Cheddar cheese

Trim off large leaves of broccoli and cut off stalk about 3 inches from bottom of floret buds. Cook broccoli, covered, in a small amount of water for 10 to 15 minutes, or until desired tenderness. Drain and cut into pieces. Arrange half of broccoli in a shallow 1½-quart baking dish. Preheat oven to 350° F. Combine soup and milk; spread half of soup mixture over broccoli, and sprinkle with half the saltine crumbs and 1 cup cheese. Repeat broccoli, soup mixture, and saltine layers. Bake, uncovered, for 25 minutes; sprinkle with remaining ½ cup cheese, and continue baking 5 minutes.   YIELD: 6 SERVINGS

NOTE: 4 cups frozen chopped broccoli, cooked according to package directions, may be substituted for fresh.

Is there anything better than a good casserole? Even the name sort of smacks of comfort. In the South, casseroles are used for every occasion—for funerals, family reunions, church socials, bridge parties. But particularly funerals. When poppa daddy finally croaks at 103, he'll be missed, but all the delicious casseroles you get from friends and neighbors helps to ease the sadness of the occasion.

Note: If you haven't been feeling well and you look out your window and notice that all the neighbor ladies up and down the street happen to be in their kitchens whipping up casseroles, you have reason to be alarmed!

FANNIE
FLAGG'S
ORIGINAL
WHISTLE STOP
CAFE
COOKBOOK
•
82

Cabbage

Use a little

2

1

1

Pe...   ...re
using a   to
quarters,

Saut   r
medium-h   l
salt; bring
onion, if d   ...to 20 minutes or unt   ...TO 6 SERVINGS

NOTE: If desired, omit salt pork and oil. After cabbage is cooked in
plain salted water, drain and stir in 1 tablespoon margarine.

(Handwritten card, numbered ③)

Oven 325°, Grease 9" sq. pan

Bowl - mix flour, soda, salt

Mixer - butter, sugars,

Add - eggs & vanilla

Add - dry ingred.

Stir in - choc. chips

Microwave - caramels + cream
Stir every 20 sec, takes (2 min.)

Glazed Carrots

2 tablespoons butter or margarine
2 tablespoons sugar, brown sugar, honey, or orange marmalade
¼ teaspoon ground cinnamon (optional)
2 cups cooked carrots

Combine first 3 ingredients in a heavy medium saucepan; cook over medium heat, stirring constantly, until melted. Add carrots and simmer 2 to 3 minutes or until hot. **YIELD: 4 SERVINGS**

Southern Fried Corn

6 ears fresh corn
½ cup milk
½ cup water
1 teaspoon sugar
2 tablespoons bacon drippings
Salt and pepper

Remove corn husks, breaking off stems. Remove silks with a stiff vegetable brush, and wash ears in cold water. To cut kernels from cob, hold corn in a large shallow bowl or dish with one hand and use a very sharp knife to cut off a thin layer from tops of kernels. Then cut down cob again one or two times, scraping remaining parts of kernels and juices into bowl. Stir in milk, water, and sugar.

FANNIE
FLAGG'S
ORIGINAL
WHISTLESTOP
CAFE
COOKBOOK
•
84

Heat bacon drippings in a large heavy skillet over medium heat; add corn mixture, and cook 10 to 12 minutes, stirring often. Remove from heat, and stir in salt and pepper to taste.
YIELD: 4 TO 6 SERVINGS

NOTE: Starches from fresh-picked summer corn will thicken this dish as it cooks. If the cooked corn is not thickened, mix 2 teaspoons flour and 2 tablespoons water until smooth; stir into skillet. Cook, stirring constantly, just until thickened.

VARIATION: If fresh corn is not available, use one 1-pound bag (2½ cups) frozen, thawed white shoepeg corn. Combine corn, ½ cup milk, ½ cup water and 1 teaspoon sugar in a saucepan; bring to a boil, and cook 5 minutes. Remove from heat; measure out 1½ cups corn and ½ cup liquid. Add 1 tablespoon all-purpose flour to corn mixture; process in an electric blender until coarsely puréed. Return to saucepan, and stir in 1 to 2 tablespoons bacon drippings, if desired. Cook over medium heat 5 minutes, stirring often. Remove from heat, and stir in salt and pepper to taste.   **YIELD: 4 TO 6 SERVINGS**

Corn Casserole

This casserole tastes like sweet creamed cornmeal mush. It's good, good, good!

- 1 17-ounce can white cream-style corn
- 1 11-ounce can white shoepeg or whole kernel corn, drained
- 1 8-ounce carton sour cream
- 2 eggs, beaten
- ½ cup margarine, melted and cooled
- 1 8½-ounce box corn muffin mix

Preheat oven to 350° F. Combine first 5 ingredients, mixing well. Stir in corn muffin mix. Pour into a greased 12- × 8- × 2-inch baking dish and bake for 45 minutes.   **YIELD: 9 TO 12 SERVINGS**

A typical day in the life of a cafe: You are hungry, you walk in and sit down, usually at a Formica table with Naugahyde chairs of red or green. Pretty soon, your waitress comes over, takes a swipe at the table with a wet rag, talking all the time: "Hi, hon. That pot roast Jesse made this morning is still good if you want some and the vegetables I have left are the greens and the potatoes and the lima beans. And I think there's still a piece of that cherry cobbler back there for you. He's got a few pieces of chicken left back there too, but they're nothing but little skimpy backs and thighs. The Jaycee's were here earlier and ate all the good pieces."

That kind of dialogue, meaning that kind of care and service, is hard to find and it seems to decline as the price of food increases.

FANNIE
FLAGG'S
ORIGINAL
WHISTLESTOP
CAFE
COOKBOOK
•
86

How to Cook Fresh Beans and Peas: Limas, Butter Beans, Crowder Peas, Black-Eyed Peas, Field Peas, Lady Peas

If you can't get crowder peas, substitute black-eyed peas.

    4   cups shelled beans or peas
    2   ounces salt pork, cubed, or drippings from 3 slices
        cooked bacon
    1   teaspoon salt

Wash shelled beans or peas and place in a large heavy saucepan. Add water to cover; bring to a boil, and skim top. Add salt pork or drippings and salt; cover, reduce heat, and simmer 30 minutes to 1 hour, or until tender. To prevent beans from being mushy, add more water during cooking, if necessary, to keep beans barely covered at all times.   **YIELD: 6 TO 8 SERVINGS**

"Congratulations to Stump Threadgoode for winning the first prize at the school Science Fair, with his project, 'The Lima Bean . . . What Is It?'"

Fresh Green Beans

Make sure you get all the strings off.

  2 pounds fresh snap, pole, or string beans
  2 ounces salt pork
  1 teaspoon salt
  1 medium onion, peeled
  1 medium russet potato, peeled

Break tips off both ends of beans; wash and drain. Cut an "x" in top of salt pork, cutting to but not through rind. Combine beans, salt pork, salt, onion, and potato in a large heavy saucepan; add water to barely cover. Bring to a boil; cover, reduce heat, and simmer 1 hour.   **YIELD: 6 TO 8 SERVINGS**

NOTE: If desired, arrange 12 new potatoes (small red potatoes), unpeeled, on top of beans during last 30 minutes of cooking time.

FANNIE
FLAGG'S
ORIGINAL
WHISTLESTOP
CAFE
COOKBOOK
•
88

Green Bean Casserole

1   10¾-ounce can cream of mushroom soup, undiluted
½   cup milk
4½   cups cooked and drained cut green beans
½   cup slivered almonds, lightly toasted (optional)
1   cup crushed saltines
1½   cups (6 ounces) shredded Cheddar cheese

Preheat oven to 350° F. Combine soup and milk. Arrange half of green beans in bottom of a greased shallow 1½-quart baking dish. Spread half of soup mixture over beans; sprinkle with half of almonds, saltines, and 1 cup cheese. Repeat bean, almond, soup mixture, and saltine layers. Bake, uncovered, for 25 minutes; sprinkle with remaining ½ cup cheese and continue baking 5 minutes longer. **YIELD: 6 SERVINGS**

Southern Turnip Greens

The cooking juice from the greens is called "pot liquor" and is served as a soup. Dip cornbread into it. It is one of the best things you will ever taste.

> 2 pounds fresh turnip greens
> 2 ounces salt pork, diced
> 1 teaspoon salt
> 1 teaspoon sugar

Break off large turnip green stems below the leaf and discard yellow or wilted leaves. Wash well by plunging greens up and down in sink or large bowl filled with water. Rinse sink or bowl to remove sand before refilling; repeat procedure several times. Drain in a colander; cut greens in half.

Combine 2 quarts water, salt pork, salt, and sugar in a large heavy saucepan; bring to a boil. Add greens; cover, reduce heat, and simmer 1 to 2 hours or until as tender as you like. Serve in bowls with some of the "pot likker" and some cornbread crumbled in each bowl. Or drain and place in a serving bowl.

YIELD: 4 SERVINGS

NOTE: If turnip greens have roots attached, peel and cut them into 1-inch cubes. Add to greens during last 45 minutes of cooking time, making sure they are covered with cooking liquid.

COLLARDS: Prepare collard greens as directed for turnip greens, except cut out center veins of greens before cooking, as they are older greens and not as tender as turnip greens.

FANNIE
FLAGG'S
ORIGINAL
WHISTLE STOP
CAFE
COOKBOOK
•
90

Buttered Okra

I am told that okra is an acquired taste, like scotch or caviar. You either love it or hate it. No contest: I love it. Fried okra, in particular, but I must admit there is nothing better than a plate of hot steaming boiled okra with its little white peas inside staring up at you. I know someone who loved it so much he named his first daughter Okra. Good thing my father didn't name me; I might have been called Budweiser.

When trimming the okra, be careful not to cut into the pod, because this will tend to make the okra slimy.

1	pound fresh whole okra
1	teaspoon salt
1	teaspoon distilled white vinegar
3	tablespoons butter or margarine, melted
2	teaspoons lemon juice

Wash okra well. Drain and cut off stem ends. Combine okra, salt, vinegar, and water to cover in a large saucepan; bring to a boil. Reduce heat and simmer 6 to 10 minutes, or until tender. Drain and place in a serving bowl; toss with butter and lemon juice. **YIELD: 4 SERVINGS**

"Idgie says that Sipsey, her colored woman, grew a stalk of okra six feet, ten inches tall, in the garden over by the Threadgoode place, and that she has that over at the cafe."

Fried Okra

This is fun to eat! Like popcorn!!

1 pound fresh okra
Self-rising flour
Vegetable oil
Salt

Wash okra well. Drain and cut off tips and stem ends; cut into
½-inch slices and place in a large bowl. Sprinkle a little water over
okra, and toss. (Okra needs to be damp for flour to adhere.) Sift
flour over okra, tossing to coat well. Toss frequently as other
batches are frying. When you are ready to cook, lift okra in batches
with hands or a slotted spoon, allowing excess flour to fall back
into bowl and setting okra on a plate. Deep-fry in hot oil (375° F.)
until browned. Do not crowd okra in the pan or it will turn mushy
and not brown properly. Transfer to a colander and drain. (Do not
drain on paper towels. Paper towels make the okra soggy.) Sprinkle
salt over okra, if desired. **YIELD: 4 SERVINGS**

FANNIE
FLAGG'S
ORIGINAL
WHISTLESTOP
CAFE
COOKBOOK
•
92

Creamed Onions

    6   medium onions, peeled and cut into ½-inch slices
    ¼   cup plus 1 tablespoon margarine, melted
    3   tablespoons self-rising flour
   1½   cups milk
    ½   teaspoon salt
    ¼   teaspoon pepper
    1   cup (4 ounces) shredded Cheddar cheese (optional)

Sauté onion in margarine in a medium saucepan over medium-high until tender. Reduce heat to medium; sprinkle flour over onion and stir until smooth. Cook 1 minute, stirring constantly. Gradually add milk, stirring until smooth; stir in salt and pepper. Cook, stirring constantly, until thickened. Stir in cheese until melted, if desired. Pour into a serving bowl. Serve with roast, meatloaf, or hamburger steaks and biscuits or grits, of course. **YIELD: 6 TO 8 SERVINGS**

Southerners will forgive anybody anything if they have good manners. Once a particularly charming Congressman who had been a guest at a church dinner my mother had attended was caught sometime later rather, well, flagrantly, as the French would say, in a motel room wearing a dog collar and his wife's lace bra and panties. Mother's response when asked if she would vote for him again? "Why, of course. After all, everybody's got their little quirks. Besides, he has lovely table manners."

Fried Onion Rings or Zucchini

Use yellow cornmeal if you can find it. East of the Mississippi, the favored color is white. The closer you get to Texas, the easier it is to find yellow in supermarkets.

Don't drain on paper towels; the fried food will get soggy. Also, try not to stack them tightly. Air needs to circulate around fried food so it will remain crisp.

- 2 cups self-rising flour
- ⅔ cup cornmeal
- ½ teaspoon salt
- ½ teaspoon pepper
- 1¾ cups milk
- 1 egg, beaten
- 6 large onions, peeled, cut into ¼-inch slices, and separated into rings, or 6 large zucchini, cut into ½-inch slices

Vegetable oil

Combine first 4 ingredients in a large bowl; beat in milk and egg. Let stand 5 minutes. Add onion or zucchini slices to batter in batches and toss with hands until vegetables are well coated. When you are ready to fry them, pick up vegetables, allowing excess batter to slide back into bowl. Place slices immediately in hot oil (375° F.), and deep-fry until browned, turning once. Drain in a colander, and sprinkle with additional salt, if desired. **YIELD: 8 SERVINGS**

FANNIE
FLAGG'S
ORIGINAL
WHISTLESTOP
CAFE
COOKBOOK
•
94

Creamed Peas

I love these with ham.

   2   tablespoons butter or margarine
   1½ tablespoons all-purpose flour
   ½   cup milk
   1   17-ounce can Le Sueur peas, undrained
   ¼   teaspoon salt

Melt butter in a small saucepan over medium-low heat; add flour and cook 1 minute, stirring constantly. Stir in milk until smooth; add peas and their liquid and salt. Cook, stirring constantly, until thickened.   **YIELD: 3 SERVINGS**

Timing is the secret to life and cooking. I admire and am in awe of cooks who can keep three burners going, four things in the oven, all to be ready at different times, and can still entertain people in the kitchen while they are cooking, and raising children, feeding dogs and cats, talking to people on the phone, know what day it is and set the table at the same time. I don't know how they do it. And they let men run the world! When I cook I must be totally alone, armed with timers, have everything written down, and if some poor soul happens to wander in the kitchen to talk to me I go to pieces. Even when things go right, I have been known to put dinner on the table, sit down and eat, and forget to serve the bread that's still in the oven, or the salad that is still in the refrigerator, sitting alongside the casserole I made earlier.

Mashed Potatoes

    4   medium potatoes (about 1¾ pounds), peeled
         and quartered
   ½   cup milk
   ¼   cup butter
 1½   teaspoons salt
   ¼   teaspoon pepper

Cook potatoes in boiling water covered for 15 minutes, or until tender. Pour off water, leaving potatoes in saucepan; return to heat and shake over heat briefly to evaporate water. Remove from pan and mash with a potato masher. Add next four ingredients and mash well. Serve hot.   **YIELD: 4 SERVINGS**

Mashed Potato Patties

I like these for breakfast.

   1   recipe mashed potatoes (page 96)
  ½   cup self-rising flour
  ¼   cup finely minced onion
  1   egg, beaten
Bacon drippings or vegetable oil

Allow mashed potatoes to cool. Stir in flour, onion, and egg, mixing well. Drop ¼ cup of potato mixture at a time into ⅛ inch of hot bacon drippings in a heavy skillet; press into ¾-inch-thick rounds with the back of a spatula or fork. Fry until golden brown, turning once. Drain well.   **YIELD: 1 DOZEN**

FANNIE
FLAGG'S
ORIGINAL
WHISTLE STOP
CAFE
COOKBOOK
•
96

Scalloped Potatoes

2 pounds russet potatoes
3 tablespoons bacon drippings
3 tablespoons margarine
1 tablespoon all-purpose flour
Salt and pepper
½ cup whipping cream
Milk

Preheat oven to 350° F. Peel potatoes and cut into very thin slices. Melt together bacon drippings and margarine. Arrange a single layer of potatoes in bottom of a greased shallow 1½-quart baking dish. Drizzle with some of the bacon drippings and margarine, and sprinkle lightly with some of the flour, salt, and pepper. Repeat layers using remaining ingredients except cream and milk. Pour cream over potatoes; add milk, if necessary, to barely cover potatoes. Cover loosely with aluminum foil; bake at 350° F. for 1¼ to 1½ hours, or until potatoes are tender. Uncover, raise oven temperature to 400° F, and bake 10 to 15 minutes or until potatoes are browned on top. **YIELD: 6 SERVINGS**

VARIATION: Scalloped potatoes with ham. Layer ½ cup minced Smithfield or country ham with the potatoes.

All you need to open a successful cafe is a love of people, good food, and a room full of tables and chairs. Mr. and Mrs. McMichael's Irondale cafe is a perfect example. I love to go to their cafe and read the paper and have a meal. There's something about being in a roomful of friendly people that softens all the bad news in all the headlines from all around the world.

Candied Yams

>   3 pounds medium-size sweet potatoes
>   1 cup sugar
> 1½ tablespoons cornstarch
> 1½ cups water
>   2 teaspoons vanilla
>   ½ cup firmly packed brown sugar
>   ½ teaspoon ground cinnamon
> Miniature marshmallows (optional)

Scrub sweet potatoes and cook in boiling water covered 25 to 40 minutes or just until tender (do not overcook). Rinse under cold water to stop cooking process; drain on paper towels. Peel and set aside.

Combine sugar and cornstarch in a small saucepan; stir in water until smooth. Cook over medium heat until thickened, stirring constantly until sugar melts. Remove from heat and stir in vanilla.

Preheat oven to 350° F. Cut potatoes into chunks or slices and arrange in a single layer in a greased shallow 2-quart baking dish. Pour sugar mixture evenly over potatoes. Combine brown sugar and cinnamon; sprinkle evenly on top. Bake for 30 minutes. If desired, drop some marshmallows over potatoes after 20 minutes of baking time. **YIELD: 8 SERVINGS**

FANNIE
FLAGG'S
ORIGINAL
WHISTLESTOP
CAFE
COOKBOOK
•
98

Sweet Potato Croquettes

These are so good with ham or pork chops!

1½	pounds sweet potatoes
2	tablespoons margarine, melted
⅓	cup firmly packed light brown sugar
½	teaspoon ground cinnamon
1	teaspoon vanilla extract
8	large marshmallows
2	cups crushed cornflakes

Scrub sweet potatoes; cook in boiling water 45 minutes to 1 hour, or until tender. Drain well and let stand until cool enough to handle. Peel and mash; stir in next 4 ingredients. Cover and refrigerate until chilled.

Form croquettes, shaping scant ⅓ cup sweet potato mixture around each marshmallow. Roll in cornflakes, pressing lightly to form 2-inch-thick patties. Deep-fry in batches in hot oil (375° F.) until browned; drain. **YIELD: 8**

My mother told me, "Honey, have your nervous breakdown early in life and you'll never regret it!" I remember the day my mother announced she was never going to cook again. She said the reason was that earlier that very morning she had experienced a complete nervous breakdown and the sounds of pots and pans made her entirely too nervous to cook, so we went out to eat. We have ever since. It was a wonderful life after that day. Mother never had to cook or clean or do a thing that was the least bit stressful. No loud noises, no upsetting news, just Bingo games and peaches and cream. I am winding up to have my breakdown any day now.

Sweet Potato Casserole

3 pounds sweet potatoes
½ cup butter or margarine
½ cup firmly packed brown sugar
¼ cup sugar
2 teaspoons vanilla extract
½ teaspoon ground cinnamon
½ teaspoon ground nutmeg
Large marshmallows

Scrub sweet potatoes and cook in boiling water covered for 40 to 50 minutes, or until fork-tender. Drain and rinse under cold water to stop cooking process; drain on paper towels. Peel when cool enough to handle; mash with margarine. Beat in next 5 ingredients with an electric mixer. Spread in a shallow greased 1½-quart baking dish and bake in a preheated 350° F. oven for 20 minutes. Cover top with marshmallows; bake 10 to 15 additional minutes or until marshmallows are melted and lightly browned. **YIELD: 6 TO 8 SERVINGS**

FANNIE
FLAGG'S
ORIGINAL
WHISTLESTOP
CAFE
COOKBOOK
•
100

Yellow Squash

    2 pounds yellow summer squash, sliced
    1 cup chopped onion
    1 cup water
    ½ teaspoon salt
    ¼ cup butter or margarine
    Pepper to taste

Combine first 4 ingredients in a large saucepan and bring to a boil. Reduce heat to medium; cook, uncovered, 15 to 20 minutes or until squash is tender, stirring frequently. Drain well in a colander; transfer to a bowl, and use a potato masher to mash coarsely with butter and pepper.   YIELD: 4 SERVINGS

Squash Croquettes

These are light and tasty and fun to eat!!

    1 recipe cooked Yellow Squash (page 101)
    2 eggs, separated
    1 cup finely crushed saltines
    ½ cup self-rising flour
    Vegetable oil

Combine squash, egg yolks, saltines, and flour; mix well. Beat egg whites until stiff but not dry; fold into squash mixture. Drop by heaping tablespoons into hot oil (375° F.), and deep-fry until golden brown. Drain in a colander.   YIELD: ABOUT 1½ DOZEN

Squash Casserole

I like to throw in a few chopped water chestnuts and onion sometimes, just for a change.

> 1   recipe cooked Yellow Squash (page 101)
> 1   cup (4 ounces) shredded Cheddar cheese
> 1   cup crushed saltines
> 2   eggs, slightly beaten

Preheat oven to 350° F. Combine all ingredients, mixing well. Pour into a greased shallow 1½-quart baking dish and bake for 35 minutes.   **YIELD: 4 TO 6 SERVINGS**

I love squash. I love the names of squash—summer squash, butternut squash, crookneck squash, yellow squash. I love a squash casserole. I don't know why my friend Norma, one of the best cooks in Alabama, laughed when she asked what I wanted for my birthday and I told her. I wasn't kidding. I think the earrings are darling but I'd rather have had the casserole.

FANNIE
FLAGG'S
ORIGINAL
WHISTLESTOP
CAFE
COOKBOOK
•
102

Zucchini Sour Cream Casserole

6   medium zucchini (about 2 pounds), cut into
    ½-inch slices
1   8-ounce carton sour cream
2   tablespoons margarine
1   cup (4 ounces) shredded sharp Cheddar cheese
½   teaspoon seasoned salt
¼   teaspoon pepper
½   cup crushed saltines or fine dry breadcrumbs

Cook zucchini in boiling salted water covered for 10 to 15 minutes or until tender. Drain well. Preheat oven to 350° F. Combine sour cream and margarine in a small saucepan and cook over medium-low heat until margarine melts, stirring constantly. Remove from heat; stir in cheese, seasoned salt, and pepper. Layer half of zucchini, sour cream mixture, and cracker crumbs in a greased shallow 1½-quart casserole; repeat layers. Bake for 20 to 25 minutes, or until hot.   **YIELD: 6 SERVINGS**

Before mother had her famous breakdown, daddy bought her a spanking new modern wall oven. A very old country woman who had been a friend of my grandmother's came to visit one day, and as she walked through the kitchen she exclaimed in delight, "Oh look, Marion, you've got your TV in the kitchen." Mother didn't have the heart to tell her that she was looking at the oven door. But that window might as well have been a TV set for all the use my mother would put it to. She didn't need a self-cleaning oven; she never got it dirty.

Stewed Tomatoes

¼ cup butter or margarine

2 to 3 tablespoons sugar

4 pounds ripe summer tomatoes, peeled and quartered

½ to 2 teaspoons salt

Pepper to taste

Soft breadcrumbs (optional)

Combine butter and sugar in a large heavy skillet; cook over medium heat until melted and golden. Add tomatoes and salt, stirring well; cover, reduce heat, and cook 20 minutes or until tender, stirring occasionally. Add pepper to taste. Thicken with soft breadcrumbs, if desired.   **YIELD: 6 TO 8 SERVINGS**

Old-Fashioned Macaroni and Cheese

This is more like a macaroni and cheese custard.

2 cups milk

3 tablespoons margarine, melted

2 tablespoons all-purpose flour

½ teaspoon salt

½ teaspoon pepper

3 eggs, beaten

5 cups cooked elbow macaroni

2½ cups (10 ounces) shredded Cheddar cheese

¾ cup fresh breadcrumbs or cracker crumbs

Preheat oven to 350° F. Combine first 6 ingredients in a bowl; beat until smooth using a wire whisk. Layer half of cooked

FANNIE
FLAGG'S
ORIGINAL
WHISTLE STOP
CAFE
COOKBOOK
•
104

macaroni in bottom of a greased 9-inch square baking dish; sprinkle with 1⅔ cups cheese and layer remaining macaroni on top. Pour milk mixture over macaroni; sprinkle with bread-crumbs. Bake, uncovered, for 50 minutes; sprinkle with remaining cheese and continue baking 5 minutes longer, or until set. **YIELD: 6 TO 8 SERVINGS**

A smile is such a little thing and it is slowly fading from our country. I notice it the most in airports. In the Deep South people will still smile at you, but as you change planes as far north as Atlanta, or as far west as Dallas, the people in those now bustling cities are beginning to get the hurried worried hassled look and are forgetting to smile back at people. It seems nowadays everyone is a stranger. I remember when my mother would come to visit me in California. By the time she arrived, I had to meet almost everyone on the plane she had made friends with, including the pilot. She never met a stranger, and her smile brightened many a day and changed many a bad mood including mine.

   She was a sweetie pie and I miss her.

BREADS

*I*t says in the Bible that "man cannot live by bread alone." I don't know about man, but I could.

FANNIE
FLAGG'S
ORIGINAL
WHISTLE STOP
CAFE
COOKBOOK
•
108

Beaten Biscuits

Unless you, like the cooks in bygone days, have a 2-foot-thick, sturdy butcher block table to pound these on, the time to beat them, and the inclination to do so, you will most likely appreciate this modern update.

  2½ cups all-purpose flour
  ¾ teaspoon sugar
  ½ teaspoon baking powder
  ¾ teaspoon salt
  ½ cup lard or vegetable shortening
  7 to 9 tablespoons ice water

Insert steel blade in food processor bowl. Add flour, sugar, baking powder, and salt, and pulse until well blended. Add lard; process until mixture resembles coarse meal. With processor running, add 7 tablespoons water in a steady stream through food chute until dough forms a ball, adding more water if necessary. Process an additional 2 minutes.

Preheat oven to 400° F. Roll dough on a floured surface to ¼-inch thickness. Cut into 1½-inch rounds. Place biscuits on an ungreased cookie sheet and prick top of each biscuit 3 times with a fork. Bake for 20 minutes, or until lightly browned.
YIELD: ABOUT 3½ DOZEN

I love biscuits first thing in the morning. When I open one up to butter, it just seems to look back up at me and say good morning!

Buttermilk Biscuits

For a crustier biscuit, place the rounds one inch apart on baking sheet. This allows the biscuits to brown slightly all the way around. If you like soft edges, place them close together on baking sheet.

2 cups self-rising flour
2 teaspoons sugar
1½ teaspoons baking powder
¾ cup buttermilk
¼ cup vegetable oil

Combine first 3 ingredients in a bowl and make a well in center. Combine buttermilk and oil; add all at once to dry ingredients and stir until dough is moist but not sticky.

Preheat oven to 450° F. Turn dough out onto a lightly floured surface and knead lightly 4 or 5 times. Roll dough to ½-inch thickness; cut with a 2-inch biscuit cutter. Knead scraps 2 or 3 times and cut as before. Place on a lightly greased baking sheet and bake for 10 minutes, or until lightly browned. Brush with melted margarine if desired.   YIELD: ABOUT 1 DOZEN

NOTE: Biscuit dough may be wrapped and refrigerated up to 3 days before shaping and baking.

"Okay. You can look now.'

When Mrs. Threadgoode saw what she had on her plate, she clapped her hands, as excited as a child on Christmas. There before her was a plate of perfectly fried green tomatoes and fresh cream-white corn, six slices of bacon, with a bowl of baby lima beans on the side and four huge light and fluffy buttermilk biscuits."

"Cleo was kinda quiet. He wasn't the one I wanted at first, but I was the one he wanted. He said he made up his mind the first night he came back home from college and saw me out in the kitchen helping Sipsey cut the biscuits on that big white tin table.

He walked into the parlor, where Momma and Poppa Threadgoode were, and he said, 'I'm going to marry that big girl out in the kitchen cuttin' biscuits.'"

FANNIE
FLAGG'S
ORIGINAL
WHISTLE STOP
CAFE
COOKBOOK
•
110

Cream Biscuits

These taste as good as they sound.

    2 cups self-rising flour
    1 cup plus 2 teaspoons whipping cream

Preheat oven to 450° F. Combine ingredients, stirring with a fork until flour is moistened. Turn dough out on a lightly floured surface; knead 4 or 5 times, and roll out to ½-inch thickness. Cut with a 2-inch biscuit cutter without twisting cutter. Place on an ungreased baking sheet and bake for 10 to 12 minutes, or until lightly browned. Brush tops with melted margarine, if desired.   **YIELD: 1 DOZEN**

NOTE: Biscuits may be made with 2¼ cups self-rising flour and 1 cup half-and-half, following same directions.

Garlic Cheese Biscuits

These biscuits are so cheesy when they are hot that you don't need to split and butter them.

    2   cups buttermilk baking mix, such as Bisquick
    ⅜   teaspoon garlic powder
    1   cup (4 ounces) shredded sharp Cheddar cheese
    ⅔   cup milk
    ¼   cup butter, melted

Preheat oven to 425° F. Combine baking mix and ¼ teaspoon of the garlic powder; mix in cheese. Add milk, stirring just until dry ingredients are moistened. Roll or pat dough on a lightly floured surface to ½-inch thickness; cut with a 1½-inch cutter. Place on a lightly greased baking sheet. Combine melted butter and the remaining ⅛ teaspoon of the garlic powder; brush on tops of biscuits, and bake for 10 minutes, or until golden.

YIELD: 1 DOZEN

Spoonbread

Real spoonbread should be soft: Like a soufflé, it waits for no one.

    2 cups milk
    ⅔ cup white cornmeal
    1 teaspoon salt
    1 teaspoon baking powder
    1 teaspoon sugar
    1 tablespoon butter or margarine
    3 eggs, separated

Preheat oven to 350° F. Scald milk in a medium saucepan. Combine cornmeal, salt, baking powder, and sugar; gradually stir mixture into scalded milk and bring just to a boil, stirring constantly. Remove from heat; stir in butter. Beat egg yolks until thick in a small mixing bowl; stir in one-fourth of hot mixture, then stir yolk mixture into remaining cornmeal mixture. Beat egg whites until stiff peaks form. Fold them into cornmeal mixture, and pour into a well-greased 1½- to 2-quart baking dish. Bake for 25 to 30 minutes, or until puffed and lightly browned. Serve immediately.   YIELD: 6 SERVINGS

Old-Fashioned Cornbread

I swear, this is the best I've ever tasted.

    4 cups cornmeal
    2 teaspoons baking soda
    2 teaspoons salt
    4 eggs, beaten
    4 cups buttermilk
  ½ cup bacon drippings, melted

Preheat oven to 450° F. Combine dry ingredients and make
a well in center. Combine eggs, buttermilk, and bacon drippings,
mixing well; add to cornmeal mixture and beat until smooth.
Heat a well-greased 12-inch cast-iron skillet in the preheated
oven until very hot. Pour batter into hot skillet; bake for 35 to 45
minutes, or until a knife inserted in center comes out clean and
top is golden brown. **YIELD: 8 TO 10 SERVINGS**

I don't know much about psychology, all I know is that when
I am very upset, I turn to eating food I used to eat as a child.
Too bad they don't serve it in bars—I could slam into
some cocktail lounge, sling my purse on the table, and
bark out, "Give me a double turnip greens with a cornbread
chaser on the side. And be quick about it!"

FANNIE
FLAGG'S
ORIGINAL
WHISTLE STOP
CAFE
COOKBOOK
•
112

Crackling Cornbread

Cracklings are bits of skin and fat rendered from pork. In the South we can buy it in packages from Piggly Wiggly. Northerners can substitute crumbled bacon, but the taste will be somewhat different. Real connoisseurs of crackling cornbread insist it be crumbled into a large glass, topped with Vidalia onion or not, sprinkled with salt and pepper, and covered with fresh buttermilk. The less adventurous cover it with sweet milk.

¼ cup plus 2 tablespoons bacon drippings
2 cups plain cornmeal
2 teaspoons baking soda
1 teaspoon salt
2 eggs, beaten
2 cups buttermilk
¾ to 1 cup cracklings or crumbled bacon

Place ¼ cup bacon drippings in a 10-inch cast-iron skillet and heat in a 450° F. oven. Combine cornmeal, baking soda, and salt; mix well. Melt the remaining 2 tablespoons bacon drippings and combine with eggs and buttermilk. Mix well and add to cornmeal mixture. Stir until smooth; stir in cracklings. Pour into skillet and bake at 450° F. for 25 minutes, or until golden brown.

YIELD: 8 SERVINGS

Corn Pones

Corn pones are oblong shapes of simply made cornbread (ground corn into meal and water). They were introduced by Native Americans to the early settlers. We call them corn pones or corn dodgers.

2¼ cups boiling water
3 cups self-rising cornmeal mix
¼ cup plus 1 tablespoon melted bacon drippings or shortening

Preheat oven to 450° F. Grease a 10-inch cast-iron skillet with 2 tablespoons drippings. Gradually stir boiling water into cornmeal mix; add 2 tablespoons drippings and mix well. Dip hands into cool water. Shape 2-inch balls of cornmeal mixture into 3- x 2-inch pone shapes, dipping hands in cool water before shaping each. Place pones in skillet with sides lightly touching and brush tops with remaining drippings. Bake for 35 to 45 minutes, or until lightly browned. **YIELD: ABOUT 10**

FANNIE
FLAGG'S
ORIGINAL
WHISTLESTOP
CAFE
COOKBOOK
•
114

Hush Puppies

These tasty little devils got their name when cooks on overnight cooking trips would throw these at the dogs at night so they'd go to sleep. Hush puppy, nothing. Throw about ten of these at me and I'll hush up too. Great with seafood.

       2 cups white cornmeal
       3 tablespoons all-purpose flour
       1 teaspoon baking powder
       ½ teaspoon baking soda
       1 teaspoon salt
       1 large egg
       1 egg white
       1 cup buttermilk
       1 tablespoon bacon drippings or vegetable oil
       3 tablespoons finely minced onion
    Vegetable oil

Combine first 5 ingredients and mix well. Beat egg and egg white, then beat in buttermilk and bacon drippings. Add to cornmeal mixture; add onion, and stir until blended. Drop 1½-inch balls of batter by spoonfuls into deep hot oil (375° F.), a few at a time, and deep-fry 2 to 3 minutes, or until golden brown. Drain on paper towels and serve immediately.   **YIELD: 6 SERVINGS**

*I*f you are anything like me, I'm sure you are tired of reading nothing but bad news. Here are some headlines I'd like to see while standing in line at the supermarket:

OAT BRAN, THE SILENT KILLER

SMALLER PORTIONS MEAN TROUBLE DOWN THE LINE

DOCTORS DISCOVER: EATING HOT BUTTERED BISCUITS ACTUALLY GOOD FOR YOU

NONFAT COTTAGE CHEESE—IT CAN KILL YOU

103-YEAR-OLD WOMAN DECLARES: PECAN PIE WITH ICE CREAM HAS KEPT ME HEALTHY

FRIED CHICKEN, THE SECRET TO A HAPPY SEX LIFE

Dinner Rolls

I think people appreciate homemade dinner rolls. They are a rare treat nowadays, and served hot, with good fresh butter melting into their middles, they can make any meal seem homey.

3½	cups all-purpose flour
1	package active dry yeast
1¼	cup milk
¼	cup sugar
¼	cup shortening
1	teaspoon salt
1	egg

Combine flour and yeast in the large bowl of an electric mixer. Combine milk, sugar, shortening, and salt in a small saucepan; heat to 105° to 115° F., stirring until sugar melts. (Do not let mixture get too hot.) Add to flour mixture, and beat in on low speed of the electric mixer just until blended. Add egg, and beat at low speed for 30 seconds. Increase speed to high and beat 3 minutes.

Remove bowl from mixer and stir in as much of the remaining flour as you can mix in with a spoon. Knead in enough of the remaining flour to make a fairly stiff dough. Knead on a lightly floured surface for 5 to 8 minutes, or until smooth and elastic. Place in a greased bowl, turning to grease top. Cover and let rise in a warm place (85° F) for 45 to 60 minutes, or until doubled in bulk.

Punch dough down; divide in half. Cover and let stand 10 minutes. Lightly grease muffin pans. Shape dough into 1-inch balls; place 3 balls in each muffin cup. Cover and let rise in a warm place for 40 minutes, or until doubled in bulk. Bake in preheated 400° F. oven for 10 to 12 minutes or until golden.

YIELD: 2 DOZEN

FANNIE
FLAGG'S
ORIGINAL
WHISTLE STOP
CAFE
COOKBOOK

•

118

Refrigerator Yeast Rolls

Like making a batch of muffins.

1   package active dry yeast
2   cups warm water (105° to 115° F.)
¾   cup vegetable oil
¼   cup sugar
1   egg, lightly beaten
4   cups self-rising flour

Dissolve yeast in warm water in a large mixing bowl. Stir in remaining ingredients and blend well. (Dough will not be as stiff as the usual roll or bread dough.) Cover and refrigerate overnight.

Preheat oven to 425° F. Stir dough down; spoon into greased muffin cups, filling each about ¾ full. Bake for 20 to 25 minutes, or until golden brown. Remove from pans immediately, and serve hot.   **YIELD: 2 DOZEN**

Unless you must for medical reasons use margarine, I prefer fresh sweet butter. Latest news from the nutrition front backs me up. Stay tuned.

Marmalade Nut Bread

Delicious (toasted or not) spread with softened cream cheese.

    3   cups all-purpose flour
    ½   cup sugar
    1   tablespoon baking powder
    ½   teaspoon salt
    2   eggs, beaten
    1   cup milk
    ½   cup vegetable oil
    ½   cup orange marmalade
    1   tablespoon freshly grated orange rind
    1   cup chopped pecans or walnuts

Preheat oven to 350° F. Combine flour, sugar, baking powder, and salt in a large bowl. Combine remaining ingredients except pecans, mixing well. Make a well in center of flour mixture; add milk mixture, and stir just until dry ingredients are moistened. Stir in pecans. Pour into a greased and floured 9- x 5- x 3-inch loaf pan. Bake for 1 hour and 10 to 15 minutes, or until a wooden pick inserted comes out clean. Let cool in pan 10 minutes; remove from pan and let cool completely on a wire rack.
YIELD: 1 LOAF

There is no better perfume than the smell of baking bread. A real estate agent who is a friend of mine always bakes fresh bread when she is having an open house. Sells houses like crazy, she says.

FANNIE
FLAGG'S
ORIGINAL
WHISTLE STOP
CAFE
COOKBOOK
•
120

Sweet Potato Bread

This is great to take to a dinner or picnic. Or to school or work or to sneak a slice just before supper. Or just after.

2	cups all-purpose flour
1	cup sugar
1¼	teaspoons baking soda
¾	teaspoon salt
1	teaspoon ground cinnamon
½	teaspoon ground cloves
½	cup chopped pecans
½	cup raisins or an additional ½ cup chopped pecans
2	eggs, beaten
1	cup cooked, mashed sweet potatoes
½	cup vegetable oil
½	cup milk

Preheat oven to 350° F. Combine first 6 ingredients in a large bowl, stirring well. Mix in pecans and raisins. Thoroughly combine eggs, sweet potatoes, oil, and milk. Make a well in center of flour mixture; add sweet potato mixture and stir just until dry ingredients are moistened. Pour batter into a greased and floured 9- x 5- x 3-inch loaf pan. Bake for 1 hour and 10 to 15 minutes, or until a wooden pick inserted in center comes out clean. Let cool in pan 10 minutes, then remove from pan, and let cool completely on a wire rack.   **YIELD: 1 LOAF**

Tea Cakes

These are small muffinlike cakes. Serve them with butter or lemon sauce or sweetened fruit, or split and fill with sliced strawberries and top with whipped cream for a tender shortcake.

2	cups all-purpose flour
¾	teaspoon baking soda
¾	teaspoon ground cinnamon
¼	teaspoon ground nutmeg
¼	teaspoon salt
1	cup sugar
2	extra-large eggs
2	teaspoons vanilla extract
½	cup vegetable oil
¼	cup butter or margarine, melted and cooled

Preheat oven to 400° F. Combine first 5 ingredients in a large mixing bowl. Set aside. Beat sugar and eggs in a small mixing bowl until thick and lemon-colored; beat in vanilla, oil, and butter. Make a well in center of dry ingredients, add egg mixture, and stir just until flour mixture is moistened. Spoon into greased and floured muffin pans, filling two-thirds full. Bake in lower third of oven for 20 minutes, or until a wooden pick inserted in center comes out clean. Let cool in pan 1 minute; remove from pan and transfer to a cloth-lined basket to serve warm.   YIELD: 14

FANNIE
FLAGG'S
ORIGINAL
WHISTLESTOP
CAFE
COOKBOOK
•
122

$\mathscr{S}$OUPS AND $\mathscr{S}$TEWS

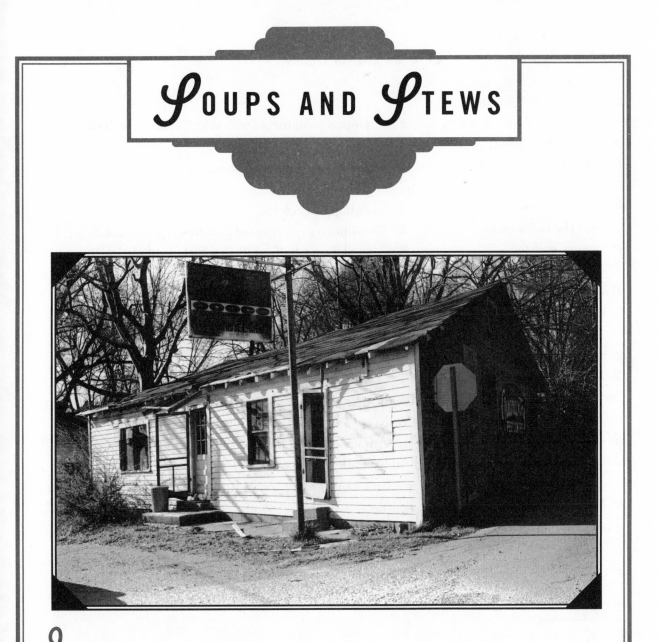

$\mathscr{I}$'m not a big fan unless soup is the whole meal. If I try to eat it early, and it is good, I always eat too much and ruin my dinner. So I like soup as my meal and a super soup served with cornbread or crackers can be plenty and delicious, especially if you are sick or it is cold outside. Chilled soup in the summer is nice too.

Oyster Stew

2   12-ounce containers fresh select oysters, including liquor
3   slices bacon, cut into 1-inch pieces
½   cup chopped onion
½   cup chopped celery
1   10½-ounce can cream of potato soup, undiluted
3   cups half-and-half, or 2 cups half-and-half and 1 cup milk
2   teaspoons Worcestershire sauce
½   teaspoon salt
½   teaspoon pepper
⅓   cup minced fresh parsley

Drain oysters, reserving liquor. Fry bacon until crisp in a large heavy saucepan. Using a slotted spoon, transfer it to paper towels to drain. Add onion and celery to bacon drippings and sauté until tender. Add soup and next 4 ingredients; bring to a boil over medium heat, stirring frequently. Add oysters and bacon and cook 3 minutes or until edges of oysters begin to curl. Sprinkle with parsley and serve. **YIELD: 6 SERVINGS**

FANNIE
FLAGG'S
ORIGINAL
WHISTLE STOP
CAFE
COOKBOOK
•
124

Vegetable Beef Soup

1½ pounds boneless beef chuck, cut into 1-inch cubes

¼ cup all-purpose flour

3 tablespoons vegetable oil

1½ quarts water

1½ teaspoons salt

1 teaspoon pepper

1 teaspoon garlic powder

4 stalks celery, sliced

2 medium onions, peeled and cut in half vertically, then sliced

1 16-ounce package frozen mixed vegetables, or ½ cup each of the following: cooked lima beans, diced carrots, cut green beans, whole kernel corn, peas, and diced potatoes

1 28-ounce can tomatoes, undrained, chopped

1 15-ounce can tomato sauce

Dredge meat in flour and brown in hot oil in a large dutch oven. Add water, salt, pepper, and garlic powder; bring to a boil. Cover, reduce heat, and simmer 1 hour. Stir in remaining ingredients; simmer, uncovered, 30 minutes to 1 hour.   **YIELD: 8 SERVINGS**

I don't know about you but the idea of meals on wheels has always appealed to me, especially if they come from the cafe. When someone was sick or could not leave the house, my Aunt Bess would send her hired man Ocie over with a hot meal. When they asked for the check, the answer was always the same: "Miss Bess says she's too busy to write one up today."

Beef Stew

This makes a lot, but leftovers taste even better.

3½ to 4 pounds boneless beef chuck, trimmed and
    cut into 1½-inch cubes
⅓ cup self-rising flour
¼ cup bacon drippings or vegetable oil
4 cups water
½ teaspoon salt
1 teaspoon seasoned salt
1 teaspoon garlic powder
1 teaspoon pepper
4 large potatoes, peeled and quartered
6 to 8 carrots, peeled and cut into 1½- to 2-inch
   pieces
3 large onions, peeled and quartered
2 14½-ounce cans whole tomatoes, undrained,
   cut up
1 15-ounce can tomato sauce

Dredge meat in flour and brown it in hot drippings in a
large dutch oven. Add water; stir in seasonings. Bring to a boil;
cover, reduce heat, and simmer for 1 hour and 15 minutes. Add
remaining ingredients; cover and simmer 40 to 45 minutes
longer. **YIELD: 10 SERVINGS**

The secret to a successful dinner party is to put plenty of
food on the table within reach. You can see when their plates
are empty and serve them right then and there. People
love to get enough to eat and often are too embarrassed
to ask for seconds. In a cafe, or a real Southern home, we
don't want anyone to feel embarrassed.

FANNIE
FLAGG'S
ORIGINAL
WHISTLE STOP
CAFE
COOKBOOK
•
126

Brunswick Stew

1   4½-pound hen
4   cups canned chicken broth or use broth from
     cooking chicken, plus more if needed
1   pound onions, peeled and sliced
1   pound red potatoes, peeled and diced
1   pound beef chuck, trimmed and cut into 1-inch
     cubes
6   slices bacon, diced
1   28-ounce can whole tomatoes, undrained,
     chopped
1   tablespoon Worcestershire sauce
1   teaspoon salt
½   teaspoon lemon pepper
½   teaspoon crushed red pepper
2   15-ounce cans butter beans, drained
2   15-ounce cans creamed corn
Hot sauce or hot pepper vinegar (optional)

Place hen in a large dutch oven and cover with water. Bring to a boil; cover, reduce heat, and simmer for 2 hours, or until tender. Remove hen from broth and cool. If desired reserve broth for stew adding water if necessary to make 4 cups. Remove skin and bones from chicken, and shred meat. Return chicken to dutch oven; add the 4 cups broth and next 9 ingredients. Bring to a boil, reduce heat, cover, and simmer for 2 hours, stirring often. Add beans and corn; cover and simmer 30 additional minutes, stirring often. Add more broth if necessary. Serve in bowls with hot sauce or vinegar, if desired.   YIELD: 10 TO 15 SERVINGS

Homemade Chili

To serve in the old-fashioned way, crumble saltines or cornbread in bottom of a bowl, then spoon chili on top. If you are planning to serve it this way, you'll need to add 1 additional cup broth or water to the chili during cooking, so you'll have plenty of liquid in the bowl to take up the crackers or bread. Add grated cheese on top if you wish.

2 pounds lean ground chuck
2 medium onions, peeled and chopped
3 cloves garlic, peeled and minced
3 cups beef broth or water
1 15-ounce can tomato sauce
1 14½-ounce can diced tomatoes, undrained
3 tablespoons uncooked oatmeal
1 teaspoon salt
1 tablespoon sugar
4 to 5 tablespoons chili powder
½ to 1 teaspoon red pepper
3 15-ounce cans pinto beans, undrained

Cook ground beef, onions, and garlic in a dutch oven until beef is browned, stirring to crumble. Drain in a colander. Return beef mixture to dutch oven and add remaining ingredients except beans, stirring well. Bring to a boil, cover, reduce heat, and simmer 40 minutes. Add beans; simmer, partially covered, 20 additional minutes. **YIELD: 6 TO 8 SERVINGS**

FANNIE
FLAGG'S
ORIGINAL
WHISTLESTOP
CAFE
COOKBOOK
•
128

SALADS AND SNACKS

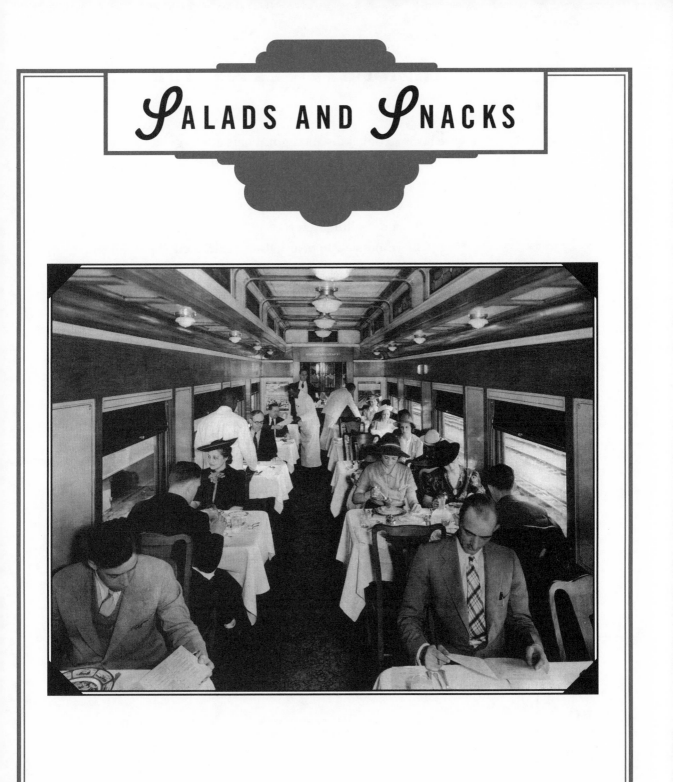

Christmas Pear Salad

This is so delicious and light. Pears are so good for you, but I hardly ever eat them, unless I have this.

1   6-ounce package lime Jello
2   cups boiling water
1   16-ounce can pear halves, undrained
2   3-ounce packages cream cheese, softened
2   tablespoons cream
8   maraschino cherries

Dissolve gelatin in boiling water. Drain pears, reserving liquid; add enough water to reserved liquid to measure 2 cups. Stir into gelatin mixture. Refrigerate until mixture has consistency of unbeaten egg white.

Meanwhile, beat cream cheese and cream until smooth. Spoon into pear halves. Spread a thin layer of gelatin in bottom of a 9-inch square baking dish; refrigerate until set but not firm. Arrange pear halves, cut sides up, in baking dish. Place a cherry in center of cream cheese mixture in each pear half. Spoon remaining gelatin over pears, and refrigerate until firm. Cut into squares and serve on lettuce.   **YIELD: 8 SERVINGS**

FANNIE
FLAGG'S
ORIGINAL
WHISTLE STOP
CAFE
COOKBOOK
•
130

Sunshine Salad

This truly tastes better than it looks. It is light, fun and
a good way to get kids to eat carrots. It tastes like sunshine!
It makes you smile.

- 1 3-ounce package lemon-flavored gelatin
- 1 cup boiling water
- 1 8¾-ounce can crushed pineapple in heavy syrup,
    undrained
- 1 cup shredded carrots
- ¼ cup chopped pecans
- Lettuce and mayonnaise

Dissolve gelatin in boiling water. Drain pineapple well, reserving syrup; add water to syrup to measure 1 cup. Stir into gelatin and chill until mixture has consistency of unbeaten egg
white. Fold pineapple, carrot, and pecans into gelatin mixture.
Pour into a 9- **x** 5- **x** 3-inch loaf pan or 4-cup mold and chill until
firm. To serve, unmold and serve slices on lettuce leaves, topped
with a dollop of mayonnaise.   **YIELD: 6 SERVINGS**

I am a train rider, and I have ridden thousands of miles
on trains and looked into the windows of hundreds of little
railroad cafes. The people inside always look so happy
that I want to get off the train and go inside and sit down
and talk with them. I think seeing them was one of the things
that inspired me to write *Fried Green Tomatoes at the Whistle
Stop Cafe*.

Frozen Fruit Salad

Fold in ¾ cup marshmallows at the same time as the whipped cream, if you like.

  1 envelope unflavored gelatin
  ½ cup boiling water
  1 16-ounce can fruit cocktail in syrup, undrained
  ½ cup mayonnaise or Miracle Whip salad dressing
2½ cups sweetened whipped cream

Dissolve gelatin in boiling water. Cool slightly, then stir in fruit cocktail and mayonnaise. Refrigerate 10 minutes. Fold in whipped cream. Pour into a small loafpan or baking dish and freeze. Slice or cut into squares, and serve on lettuce.
YIELD: 4 TO 6 SERVINGS

Fruit Salad

3 large bananas, sliced
2 large Red Delicious apples, peeled and diced
½ cup chopped pecans, toasted
½ cup finely chopped celery
½ cup raisins (optional)
⅔ cup mayonnaise
¼ cup sugar

Combine all ingredients in a bowl; mix well. Cover and chill.
YIELD: 8 TO 10 SERVINGS

FANNIE
FLAGG'S
ORIGINAL
WHISTLESTOP
CAFE
COOKBOOK
•
132

Cucumber and Onion Salad

Better the next day.

    3   medium cucumbers, peeled and very thinly
        sliced
    2   medium onions, peeled, thinly sliced, and separated
        into rings
    1   cup sour cream
    1½ teaspoons seasoned salt
    ½   teaspoon pepper

Combine all ingredients; cover and refrigerate 2 hours before serving.   **YIELD: 6 SERVINGS**

Potato Salad

In the South, mayonnaise is really Miracle Whip to older folks. For instance, if I asked my grandmother for a sandwich with mayonnaise on it, I'd get Miracle Whip. But you use what you like.

 6 medium potatoes
 3 hard-cooked eggs, peeled and chopped
 1 small onion, peeled and finely minced (optional)
 1 cup finely chopped celery
 ½ cup finely chopped green pepper
 ¾ cup mayonnaise or Miracle Whip salad dressing
 1½ teaspoons prepared mustard
 ½ teaspoon salt
 ½ teaspoon pepper

Cook potatoes in boiling water to cover for 30 minutes, or until tender. Drain and let stand until cool enough to handle. Peel and cut potatoes into cubes. Add eggs, onion if desired, celery, and green pepper. Combine remaining ingredients and toss with potato mixture. Serve immediately or refrigerate.

YIELD: 6 SERVINGS

Mother told me: "Honey, I tried all my life to please everybody and I just couldn't do it. So just do the things that please you and you will know that at least one person will be pleased!"

FANNIE
FLAGG'S
ORIGINAL
WHISTLE STOP
CAFE
COOKBOOK
•
134

Slaw

This is a must with barbecue! Or a chicken dinner.

1   1½-pound head cabbage
½   cup vegetable oil
3   tablespoons sugar
3   tablespoons cider vinegar
2   tablespoons catsup
1   tablespoon lemon juice
½   medium onion, peeled and cut into chunks
½   teaspoon salt
1   teaspoon paprika

Ask deli department to core cabbage and slice it paper-thin.
Process remaining ingredients in an electric blender until
smooth; pour over cabbage and toss well. Serve immediately, or
cover and refrigerate 1 hour before serving.   YIELD: 6 TO 8
SERVINGS

Go Ahead, Make an Aspic of Yourself

I guess the thing I love better than anything is a good tomato aspic on a hot summer day. Was there an occasion when three or four women gathered for lunch in the South when a tomato aspic was not served? If so I don't know about it. Every lunch or bridge game or garden club meeting offers some sort of congealed salad. They are so popular that in most cafes you usually have your choice of three or four different kinds of sweet salads.

My favorite thing to do in the summer is to make a couple of salads and keep them in the refrigerator to snack on for two or three days. At least that's always my plan. However, I must admit they rarely last more than one day, because snacking can really sneak up on you if you are not careful. I am reminded of the pitfalls of snacking whenever I think about my friend Squatsy's great aunt Nanny Lee. Aunty Nanny would sit on her front verandah in Mobile, Alabama and exactly at noon would have one Mint Julep on ice, just to "refresh herself". All afternoon, as she graciously entertained guests she would hand her silver cup to anyone going to the kitchen and say, "Honey, could you just sweeten my drink a little for me". By the time the sun went down Aunt Nanny was sometimes so sweetened that she had to be carried off the porch and put to bed insisting all the while that she was not at all the least bit intoxicated, "Why how could I be? After all, I just had one drink!"

I know how Aunt Nanny feels when I look in my refrigerator and my entire aspic is gone. "Why how could that be? I just had one little bite!"

FANNIE
FLAGG'S
ORIGINAL
WHISTLESTOP
CAFE
COOKBOOK
•
136

Tomato Aspic

This makes a perfect summer lunch.

3 envelopes unflavored gelatin

1 46-ounce can tomato juice

2 tablespoons grated onion

2 tablespoons sugar

1 tablespoon lemon juice

½ teaspoon salt

1 cup finely minced celery

½ cup finely minced green pepper (optional)

Lettuce leaves and mayonnaise

Sprinkle gelatin over 1½ cups tomato juice; let stand 1 minute. Cook mixture over medium heat until gelatin dissolves, stirring frequently. Stir in onion, sugar, lemon juice, salt, and remaining tomato juice. Chill until consistency of unbeaten egg white. Fold in celery and green pepper, if desired; spoon into an oiled 6-cup ring mold. Cover and chill until firm. Serve on lettuce leaves, topped with mayonnaise.   **YIELD: 10 TO 12 SERVINGS**

I've tried to follow mother's tender advice often: "Honey, I have lived high on the hog and I have lived low on the hog . . . I'll take high." I agree.

Deviled Eggs

I've never seen a more appreciated little snack—they even have a deviled egg plate just for displaying these treats!

 1 dozen hard-cooked eggs
 1 5-ounce jar pasteurized Neufchâtel cheese spread
     with olives, or pimiento-flavored
 2 tablespoons mayonnaise
 2 tablespoons minced sweet pickles
 2 tablespoons minced sweet onion
 ½ teaspoon salt

Peel eggs and cut in half lengthwise. Mash yolks; blend with cheese spread and mayonnaise. Stir in remaining ingredients. Refill egg whites.   **YIELD: 2 DOZEN HALVES**

FANNIE
FLAGG'S
ORIGINAL
WHISTLESTOP
CAFE
COOKBOOK
•
138

Cheese Ball

The all-American cheese ball is great for holidays, or to keep around in case of unexpected guests, or just for informal bowling on the lawn.

    4 cups (1 pound) shredded sharp Cheddar cheese
    ¾ cup mayonnaise
    1 small onion, peeled and grated
    1 cup chopped pecans
    ¼ teaspoon red pepper
    Strawberry preserves

Combine cheese, mayonnaise, and onion in a food processor; process until blended. Stir in pecans and red pepper. Shape into a mound on a serving plate; cover and refrigerate 2 hours. Spread preserves on top before serving with crackers.

YIELD: 10 TO 12 SERVINGS

Pimiento Cheese

I love a good pimiento cheese sandwich, just plain. But you can also stuff celery with this or add crumbled bacon and sliced hard-cooked eggs to the sandwich. It also tastes good in a BLT.

3 cups (12 ounces) shredded mild Cheddar cheese
1 cup mayonnaise
2 tablespoons grated onion
2 to 3 teaspoons Worcestershire sauce (optional)
¼ to ½ teaspoon red pepper
2 4-ounce jars diced pimiento, drained

Combine first 4 ingredients in a food processor; pulse until blended and cheese is processed as fine as you want it. Add pimiento; pulse just to blend. Store in covered container in the refrigerator. **YIELD: ABOUT 3 CUPS**

FANNIE
FLAGG'S
ORIGINAL
WHISTLE STOP
CAFE
COOKBOOK
•
140

DESSERTS

There are no fruitcake recipes in this book. That's for a very sound nutritional reason. I hate fruitcake. I have been and continue to be tortured and tormented with fruitcakes every Christmas. Friends that I adore send me a fruitcake every year and I am running out of people to give them to. My mailman won't take them anymore. He says he'd rather have cash. So would I. I am beginning to wonder if my friends are sending fruitcakes that someone sends them. Maybe there are only about ten fruitcakes in the world and they are just being sent all over the country like a fruitcake chain letter. Anyhow, I can see no purpose whatsoever for the stuff except for target practice or home insulation.

Also you may have noticed that there is not a single mention of the dreaded raisin in this book (well, maybe just one or two). I spent the better part of my childhood removing raisins from bread puddings, rice puddings, cereals, and cinnamon buns, and this is my revenge. You, of course, may feel free to add them to anything you desire, and God bless you.

*A*labamans are pie eaters. What kind? All kinds of pie, from little fried pies to cream pies. One of the cafe's biggest sellers is coffee and a slab of pie.

Apple Pie

Pastry for double-crust pie (page 26)
5½ cups peeled, cored, thinly sliced apples (¼ inch thick)
  1 tablespoon lemon juice
  ¾ cup firmly packed light brown sugar
  3 tablespoons all-purpose flour
  1 teaspoon ground cinnamon
  ¼ teaspoon ground ginger
  ⅛ teaspoon salt
  2 tablespoons butter or margarine
Sugar

Preheat oven to 400° F. Roll half of pastry to ⅛-inch thickness on a lightly floured surface; fit into a deep-dish 9-inch pie plate. Set aside.

Toss apples with lemon juice. Combine brown sugar, flour, spices, and salt; mix with apples. Spoon apple mixture into pastry shell; dot with butter. Roll remaining half of pastry to ⅛-inch thickness, place over apple mixture, and trim. Fold edges under, flute, and cut slits in top of pastry. Bake for 1 hour, or until apples are tender (shield edges of pastry with strips of aluminum foil, if necessary, to prevent excess browning). Sprinkle top lightly with sugar while hot, if desired; cool before cutting.
YIELD: ONE DEEP-DISH 9-INCH PIE

FANNIE
FLAGG'S
ORIGINAL
WHISTLE STOP
CAFE
COOKBOOK
•
144

Mincemeat Apple Pie

Pastry for double-crust 9-inch pie (page 26)
1   16-ounce can mincemeat
2   cups diced, peeled Granny Smith apples
2   tablespoons sugar
2   tablespoons lemon juice
½   teaspoon grated lemon rind

Preheat oven to 375° F. Roll half of pastry to ⅛-inch thickness on a lightly floured surface. Place in a 9-inch pie plate; set aside.

Combine remaining ingredients in a medium saucepan and cook over medium heat until hot, stirring frequently. Spoon into prepared pastry shell. Roll remaining pastry to ⅛-inch thickness; transfer to top of pie. Trim, fold edges, and flute. Cut slits in top crust. Bake for 30 to 40 minutes, covering edges of pastry with strips of aluminum foil to prevent excess browning, if necessary.

YIELD: ONE 9-INCH PIE

"Evelyn was still taking things out of the box. 'Look, Mrs. Hartman, here's an old menu from the Whistle Stop Cafe. It must be from the thirties. Can you believe those prices? A barbecue for ten cents . . . and you could get a complete dinner for thirty-five cents! And pie was a nickel!'"

Southern Fried Fruit Pies

Wonderful for breakfast, afternoon snack, midnight snack, anytime . . .

PASTRY

- 2 cups all-purpose flour
- 1 teaspoon baking soda
- ½ teaspoon salt
- ½ cup lard or vegetable shortening
- 2 to 3 tablespoons ice water

FILLING

- 3 cups dried apples, peaches, or apricots
- 1½ cups boiling water
- ½ cup sugar
- ¼ teaspoon ground cinnamon
- ¼ teaspoon ground allspice

Vegetable oil
Granulated or powdered sugar

First, make the pastry: Combine flour, baking soda, and salt; cut in lard with a pastry blender until mixture resembles coarse meal. Sprinkle ice water over flour mixture by tablespoonfuls, mixing lightly with a fork until enough has been added to allow dough to form a ball. Wrap ball, and chill at least 1 hour.

Cook fruit in boiling water, covered, for 30 minutes, or until very tender; cool and mash slightly. Stir in ½ cup sugar and spices.

Divide chilled pastry in half; roll each half to ¼-inch thick-

FANNIE
FLAGG'S
ORIGINAL
WHISTLE STOP
CAFE
COOKBOOK
•
146

ness and cut into 5-inch circles. Reroll scraps, and cut into circles. Place 2 to 3 tablespoons fruit mixture on half of each pastry circle; moisten edges of pastry circles and fold over filling, making sure edges meet. Press edges together, using a fork dipped in flour. Fry in deep hot oil (375° F.) until golden brown. Drain on paper towels; sprinkle with sugar while hot.   **YIELD: 10 TO 12**

NOTE: Fresh fruit may be substituted for dried. Increase amount to 4 cups and simmer, covered in a small amount of water, until tender. Mash coarsely or chop finely, and mix with sugar and spices.

My graduation dress still fits. My leg, that is. Worried about calories? You've come to the wrong cafe. Or the wrong cookbook.

FANNIE
FLAGG'S
ORIGINAL
WHISTLE STOP
CAFE
COOKBOOK
•
148

Banana Cream Pie

If you are a true banana lover this is the ultimate . . .

¾	cup plus 2 tablespoons sugar
3	tablespoons plus 1 teaspoon cornstarch
⅛	teaspoon salt
3	egg yolks, beaten
1½	cups half-and-half
1	cup milk
1	tablespoon butter or margarine
1½	teaspoons vanilla extract
2	medium bananas, peeled
2	teaspoons lemon juice
1	baked 9-inch pastry shell (page 26-make ½ recipe)
¾	cup whipping cream
⅓	cup sifted powdered sugar

Combine sugar, cornstarch, and salt in a heavy saucepan; stir well. Combine egg yolks, half-and-half, and milk and beat until blended. Gradually stir into sugar mixture until smooth. Cook over medium heat, stirring constantly, until mixture thickens and boils. Boil 1 minute, stirring constantly. Transfer to a glass bowl; stir in butter and vanilla. Cover with plastic wrap and cool to room temperature. Slice one banana and toss with 1 teaspoon lemon juice to prevent browning. Arrange the sliced banana in bottom of pastry shell. Pour cooled custard over banana, cover, and chill until firm.

Beat whipping cream and powdered sugar until stiff peaks form. Spread over pie filling. Slice remaining banana and toss with remaining 1 teaspoon lemon juice; drain juice, if any, and arrange on top of pie. **YIELD: ONE 9-INCH PIE**

COCONUT CREAM PIE: Prepare just like the Banana Cream Pie, omitting bananas and lemon juice. Instead, stir in ½ cup flaked coconut and 1 teaspoon coconut extract with the butter and vanilla. Top pie with toasted coconut.   YIELD: ONE 9-INCH PIE

This is my favorite cream pie. It's so sweet your hair will stand up on your head.

Banana Split Pie

Crushed pineapple doesn't work well in this pie, because the liquid in it makes the pie water. That is also why the tidbits are patted dry.

- ¼ cup margarine, softened
- 3 tablespoons whipping cream
- 2 cups powdered sugar
- 1 teaspoon vanilla extract
- 1 9-inch graham cracker crust
- 1 medium banana
- 1 8-ounce can pineapple tidbits, drained
- 1½ cups frozen, thawed whipped topping
- ½ cup chopped pecans
- ½ cup chopped drained maraschino cherries

Beat margarine until creamy; beat in cream and sugar until smooth. Spread in pie shell. Slice banana; chop pineapple and pat dry with paper towels. Arrange banana and pineapple on top of cream mixture, and press in firmly. Spread whipped topping on pie; sprinkle with pecans and cherries. Refrigerate 2 hours; store in refrigerator after cutting.   YIELD: ONE 9-INCH PIE

"Thank you, honey, I just love candy. I used to love Tootsie Rolls, but, you know, those things can pull your teeth out if you're not careful—a Bit-O-Honey will do the same thing."

Black Bottom Pie

Too sinful to discuss.

1¾ cups crushed chocolate wafer cookies
¼ cup butter or margarine, softened
1 envelope unflavored gelatin
1¾ cups milk
¾ cup sugar
½ teaspoon salt
1 tablespoon plus 1 teaspoon cornstarch
4 egg yolks
1½ ounces unsweetened chocolate, melted
1 teaspoon vanilla extract
2 tablespoons bourbon
1½ cups whipping cream
½ cup powdered sugar
½ cup chopped pecans

Combine cookie crumbs and butter; mix well and press on bottom and up side of a 9-inch pie plate. Chill.

Soften gelatin in ¼ cup milk. Combine sugar, salt, and cornstarch in a heavy saucepan; gradually stir in remaining 1½ cups milk until smooth. Add egg yolks and beat well. Cook over medium heat, stirring constantly, until mixture is thick. (Do not let it boil.) Remove from heat. Measure out into small bowl ¼ cup plus 1 tablespoon mixture. Stir chocolate and vanilla into reserved custard mixture and whisk until blended and cooled. Spread in pie shell and refrigerate.

Add softened gelatin to mixture in saucepan; stir until gelatin dissolves. (Return briefly to heat if necessary.) Chill until mixture begins to thicken, then stir in bourbon. Beat whipping cream and powdered sugar until stiff peaks form; fold one-third into chilled custard mixture. Spread custard mixture over firm

FANNIE
FLAGG'S
ORIGINAL
WHISTLE STOP
CAFE
COOKBOOK
•
150

chocolate mixture in the pie shell. Spread remaining whipped cream mixture over custard mixture. Sprinkle with pecans, and refrigerate 3 to 4 hours, or until set.   **YIELD: ONE 9-INCH PIE**

Butterscotch Meringue Pie

This is as old fashioned as chess pie and as good. Hardly anybody serves butterscotch anymore and I like it: don't you?

   1   cup firmly packed light brown sugar
   ¼   cup cornstarch
   ½   teaspoon salt
   3   cups half-and-half or evaporated milk
   4   eggs, separated
   2   tablespoons butter or margarine, softened
  1¾   teaspoons vanilla extract
   ½   teaspoon butter-rum extract (optional)
   1   baked 9-inch pastry shell (page 26, make ½ recipe)
   ½   teaspoon cream of tartar
   ½   cup granulated sugar

Combine brown sugar, cornstarch, and salt in a heavy, medium saucepan. Stir in half-and-half until smooth. Cook over medium heat, stirring constantly, until mixture thickens and comes to a boil. Cook 1 minute, stirring constantly. Slightly beat the egg yolks and stir in one-fourth of hot mixture, then blend yolk mixture into remaining hot mixture. Cook 1 minute, stirring constantly. Remove from heat; stir in butter, 1 teaspoon vanilla, and the butter rum extract, if you wish. Pour into pastry shell.

Preheat oven to 400° F. Beat egg whites and cream of tartar until foamy; beat in granulated sugar, 1 tablespoon at a time, beating until stiff peaks form. Beat in remaining ¾ teaspoon vanilla; spread over hot filling, sealing to edge. Bake for 15 minutes, or until meringue is lightly browned. Cool; serve warm or cold.　**YIELD: ONE 9-INCH PIE**

NOTE: The secret to making meringue is to add the sugar gradually while beating egg whites, so the sugar will dissolve. To prevent the meringue from weeping, spread over the *hot* filling before baking, and spread to edges to seal completely. All meringue will weep a little after you refrigerate the pie.

My mother and daddy had a wild raccoon that they used to feed every night. He loved ice cream, so they fixed him a bowl of vanilla ice cream with six vanilla wafers stuck all around the side of the dish. Whenever they went on a trip to see me, they fixed two weeks' worth of these bowls and my Uncle Bill came to the house every night and fed the raccoon so he would not have to go one single night without his ice cream. I am always amazed at such little acts of kindness. Lucky raccoon.

FANNIE
FLAGG'S
ORIGINAL
WHISTLESTOP
CAFE
COOKBOOK
•
152

Baked Egg Custard Pie

When I eat this, it makes me feel like I'm 12 years old again, and all's right with the world . . .

1   unbaked 9-inch pastry shell
3   eggs, beaten
1   12-ounce can evaporated milk
1   cup sugar
3   tablespoons all-purpose flour
1   teaspoon vanilla extract
½   teaspoon ground nutmeg

Bake pastry shell at 400° F. for 5 minutes; cool. Leave oven on. Combine remaining ingredients in a bowl and mix well with a wire whisk. Pour into pie shell and bake at 400° F. for 10 minutes; reduce heat to 325° F. and bake 25 to 30 minutes longer, or until a knife inserted in center comes out clean. Let cool to room temperature before serving. Store in refrigerator. **YIELD: ONE 9-INCH PIE**

Attention: Would all the men out there who can drop ten pounds in one week by just cutting down a little on their food please apologize to all the women in the world over forty. Thank you.

    P.S. Don't tell me God isn't a man.

Lemon Meringue Pie

1⅞ cups sugar
⅓ cup cornstarch
¼ teaspoon salt
2 cups milk
3 eggs, separated, plus 1 extra egg white
1½ teaspoons grated lemon rind
½ cup fresh lemon juice
2 tablespoons butter or margarine
1 baked 9-inch pastry shell (page 26, make ½ recipe)
½ teaspoon cream of tartar

Combine 1½ cups sugar, cornstarch, and salt in a heavy saucepan. Gradually add milk, stirring until blended. Cook over medium heat, stirring constantly, until thickened and mixture comes to a boil. Boil gently for 1 minute, stirring constantly. Remove from heat.

Preheat oven to 350° F. Beat egg yolks at high speed of an electric mixer until thick and lemon-colored. Gradually stir about one-fourth of hot milk mixture into yolks; add this to remaining hot mixture, stirring constantly. Cook over medium heat, stirring constantly, for 2 to 3 minutes. Remove from heat; stir in lemon rind, lemon juice, and butter, stirring until butter melts. Pour filling into baked pie shell.

Beat the 4 egg whites and cream of tartar at high speed of an electric mixer until foamy. Gradually add remaining ¼ cup plus 2 tablespoons sugar, 1 tablespoon at a time, beating until stiff peaks form. Spread meringue over hot filling, sealing to edge. Bake for 12 to 15 minutes, or until browned. Cool before cutting. **YIELD: ONE 9-INCH PIE**

FANNIE
FLAGG'S
ORIGINAL
WHISTLESTOP
CAFE
COOKBOOK
•
154

Lemon Chess Pie

Old fashioned and good.

  2 eggs
  4 egg yolks
1½ cups sugar
  ¼ cup butter or margarine, melted
  ¼ cup whipping cream
  1 tablespoon cornmeal
  1 tablespoon all-purpose flour
  ¼ cup fresh lemon juice
  1 tablespoon grated lemon rind
  1 unbaked 9-inch pastry shell

Preheat oven to 350° F. Beat eggs, egg yolks, and sugar at high speed of an electric mixer until thick and lemon-colored. Gradually add butter and cream, beating for 1 minute. Stir in cornmeal, flour, lemon juice, and lemon rind. Pour into pastry shell; bake for 40 to 45 minutes, or until set. Cool to room temperature before cutting.   **YIELD: ONE 9-INCH PIE**

People say you can never be too rich or too thin. I disagree. First of all, forget about being too rich—none of us will have to worry about that. Taxes take care of that problem. As far as trying to be too thin, in a world where people are really starving to death, I do not see where looking like one of those poor people can ever be thought of as fashionable.

Lemon Ice Box Pie

Nothing makes me happier than a wonderful slice of Lemon Ice Box Pie. It is especially good after a huge feast of barbecue.

1½   cups vanilla wafer crumbs (about 40 wafers)
¼   cup butter or margarine, melted
1   8-ounce package cream cheese, softened
1   14-ounce can sweetened condensed milk
1   6-ounce can frozen lemonade concentrate, thawed
Few drops yellow food coloring (optional)
1   4-ounce container frozen whipped topping,
     thawed, plus additional whipped topping

Combine crumbs and butter; press firmly on bottom and up sides of a 9-inch pie plate. Chill. Beat cream cheese until fluffy in a large mixing bowl; gradually beat in sweetened condensed milk, lemonade concentrate, and food coloring, if desired. Fold whipped topping in 4-ounce container; pour into pastry shell. Chill 4 hours or until set. Garnish with additional whipped topping.   **YIELD: ONE 9-INCH PIE**

FANNIE
FLAGG'S
ORIGINAL
WHISTLE STOP
CAFE
COOKBOOK
•
156

Key Lime Pie

3 egg yolks
1 14-ounce can sweetened condensed milk
½ cup concentrated lime juice or bottled key lime
   juice
Few drops green food coloring (optional)
1 9-inch graham cracker crust
2 cups sweetened whipped cream or frozen, thawed
   whipped topping

Preheat oven to 325° F. Beat first 4 ingredients in a mixing bowl until smooth. Pour into graham cracker crust; bake for 30 minutes. Cool completely; cover and chill. Spread whipped cream on top before cutting.   **YIELD: ONE 9-INCH PIE**

I feel so lucky to be living at a time when so many talented people have been around and I have enjoyed their work so much. Not just cooks and cafe owners. I wish I could pay everyone back for all the wonderful hours of entertainment and joy they have given me. If I could I would take Doris Day, Charles Kuralt, Stephen Sondheim, and Ginger Rogers out to a big dinner. I would like to take all the nurses and teachers out, too. And sit the weary waitresses right down here beside me, hon. . . .

Good Ole Pecan Pie

The age-old debate is whether to use light or dark corn syrup, and whether to use plain sugar or brown sugar. In the South we use light corn syrup. Brown sugar makes it more caramel-tasting. Serve with a scoop of vanilla ice cream.

- ½ cup butter or margarine, melted
- 1 cup firmly packed light brown sugar
- 1 cup light corn syrup
- 4 eggs, beaten
- 2 teaspoons vanilla extract
- ⅓ teaspoon salt
- 1 unbaked 9-inch pastry shell
- 1½ cups pecan halves

Preheat oven to 325° F. Combine first 3 ingredients in a small saucepan and cook over medium heat, stirring constantly, until butter melts and sugar dissolves. Cool slightly. Beat eggs, vanilla, and salt in a large bowl; gradually add sugar mixture, beating well with a wire whisk. Pour into pastry shell and scatter pecans over top. Bake for 50 to 55 minutes. Serve warm or chilled.
YIELD: ONE 9-INCH PIE

GOOD OLE PEANUT PIE: Prepare just like the Good Ole Pecan Pie, but use 1½ cups honey-roasted peanuts instead of pecans. Thank you George Washington Carver!

A balanced meal. Isn't that when you have the same amount of sugar as you do fat?

FANNIE
FLAGG'S
ORIGINAL
WHISTLE STOP
CAFE
COOKBOOK
•
158

Kentucky Bourbon
Chocolate Pecan Pie

Oh please, just hand me my girdle and another piece of
pie to go . . .

- 1 cup sugar
- 1 cup light corn syrup
- ½ cup butter or margarine
- 4 eggs, lightly beaten
- ¼ cup bourbon
- 1 teaspoon vanilla extract
- ¼ teaspoon salt
- 1 cup semisweet chocolate chips
- 1 cup pecan pieces
- 1 unbaked pastry shell fitted into a 9-inch deep-dish
  pie plate

Preheat oven to 325° F. Combine first 3 ingredients in a
small saucepan and cook over medium heat, stirring constantly,
until butter melts and sugar dissolves. Cool slightly. Beat eggs,
bourbon, vanilla, and salt in a large bowl; gradually add sugar
mixture, beating well with a wire whisk. Stir in chocolate chips
and pecans; pour into pastry shell. Bake for 50 to 55 minutes,
or until set. Serve warm or chilled.   YIELD: ONE DEEP-DISH
9-INCH PIE

Southerners love food so much they even use food as names
for their loved ones: Sweetie Pie, Sugarcakes, Honey, Honey-pie,
Honeybun, and so on. I even had an Uncle Cheese, and
my mother called me her little dumpling, even after I
grew up to be a big dumpling.

Sweet Potato or Pumpkin Pie

These are great for the holidays and football parties.

    ¼ cup butter or margarine, softened
    1 cup sugar
    2 eggs, separated
1½ cups cooked mashed sweet potatoes or pumpkin
    ¾ cup evaporated milk or half-and-half
    1 teaspoon vanilla extract
    ½ teaspoon ground cinnamon
    ½ teaspoon ground nutmeg
    ¼ teaspoon ground ginger
    1 unbaked 9-inch pastry shell
Whipped cream

Preheat oven to 350° F. Cream butter with electric mixer; gradually add ¾ cup sugar, beating well. Beat in egg yolks. Stir in sweet potatoes and next 5 ingredients. Beat egg whites until foamy. Gradually add remaining ¼ cup sugar, 1 tablespoon at a time, beating until stiff peaks form. Fold into sweet potato mixture. Pour into pastry shell and bake for 40 to 45 minutes, or until set. Cool; top with dollops of whipped cream.   **YIELD: ONE 9-INCH PIE**

FANNIE
FLAGG'S
ORIGINAL
WHISTLE STOP
CAFE
COOKBOOK
•
160

Cakes

*W*hat is it about eating outside that makes the food taste so much better? Is it our natural desire to get back to nature? I don't know about all regions, but Southerners love to eat out of doors—from picnics to backyard barbecues to church "dinners on the ground," to hamburgers by the lake or hot dogs on the beach. My favorite eating is done on a porch. Dan Martin has a wonderful old home in Georgia that has a side porch off the kitchen, with hanging wisteria, overlooking a lazy pond. I have never had better breakfasts than sitting on that little porch at sunrise watching the world slowly wake up, shake off the morning dew, and start on its way to becoming another beautiful Georgia day. My cup of hot coffee and the eggs and bacon, biscuits with fresh peach jam take on a magical taste of their own. I have been taken to some of the best restaurants in my day; I'll take Dan's side porch any time.

German Chocolate Cake

1   4-ounce package sweet baking chocolate
¼   cup water
1   cup shortening
2   cups sugar
4   eggs, separated
1   cup buttermilk
1   teaspoon baking soda
1   teaspoon vanilla extract
2½ cups sifted all-purpose flour
½   teaspoon salt
Coconut Pecan Frosting (recipe follows)

Combine chocolate and water and cook over medium heat until chocolate melts, stirring frequently. Cool.

Cream shortening with an electric mixer; gradually beat in sugar. Add egg yolks, one at a time, beating well after each addition. Add chocolate mixture, and beat until well blended.

Preheat oven to 350° F. Combine buttermilk, baking soda, and vanilla in a small bowl, mixing well. Combine flour and salt. Add flour mixture to the chocolate batter alternately with buttermilk mixture, beginning and ending with dry ingredients. Beat egg whites until stiff peaks form; fold into batter. Pour into 2 greased and floured 9-inch round cake pans. Bake for 25 to 30 minutes, or until a wooden pick inserted in center comes out clean. Let stand in pans 10 minutes; remove from pans, and cool completely on wire racks. Spread coconut pecan frosting between layers and on top and sides of cake. **YIELD: ONE 2-LAYER CAKE**

COCONUT PECAN FROSTING

1⅓   cups whipping cream
1⅓   cups sugar
  4   egg yolks, beaten
 ⅔   cup butter or margarine
  2   teaspoons vanilla extract
1⅓   cups flaked coconut
1⅓   cups chopped pecans
  2   ounces sweet baking chocolate, grated

Combine first 4 ingredients in a large heavy saucepan; cook over low heat, stirring constantly, until butter and sugar melt. Bring to a boil over medium heat and cook for 12 minutes, stirring constantly. Remove from heat; add vanilla, coconut, and pecans. Let stand until cool and of spreading consistency, stirring frequently. Stir in three-fourths of chocolate when cool. Spread between cake layers and on top and sides of cake. Sprinkle remaining grated chocolate on top.   **YIELD: ENOUGH FROSTING AND FILLING FOR A 2-LAYER CAKE**

FANNIE
FLAGG'S
ORIGINAL
WHISTLE STOP
CAFE
COOKBOOK
•
164

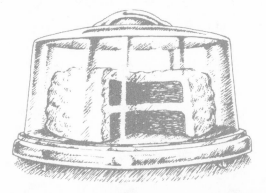

Chocolate Sheath Cake

2 cups sugar
2 cups all-purpose flour
1 teaspoon baking soda
1 teaspoon ground cinnamon
1 cup water
½ cup margarine, melted
½ cup buttermilk
½ cup vegetable oil
¼ cup cocoa
2 eggs, beaten
1 teaspoon vanilla extract
Chocolate Icing (recipe follows)

Preheat oven to 400° F. Sift sugar, flour, soda, and cinnamon into a large bowl. Whisk together remaining ingredients until smooth; add to dry ingredients and stir well. Pour into a greased and floured 13- × 9- × 2-inch baking pan. Bake for 20 minutes. Spread chocolate icing over *hot* cake; serve warm or at room temperature. **YIELD: 12 TO 16 SERVINGS**

CHOCOLATE ICING

¼ cup plus 2 tablespoons milk
¼ cup cocoa
½ cup margarine
3½ cups sifted powdered sugar
1 teaspoon vanilla extract
1 cup chopped pecans

Mix milk and cocoa until smooth in a large saucepan. Add margarine and bring to a simmer over medium heat, stirring frequently until margarine melts. Remove from heat, and stir in sugar and vanilla until smooth. Stir in pecans; spread over hot cake.

"I was already engaged to Cleo, so I must have been seventeen at the time. It was a Saturday afternoon in June, and we had just had the best time at our BYO church picnic. The young people's group from the Andalusia Baptist Church had ridden the train over for the day, and Momma and Sipsey had baked about ten coconut cakes for the occasion."

Don't You Just Love Easter?

*O*ther than Christmas and Halloween, it's my favorite holiday. I once had an Easter Egg hunt and invited about fifty friends and paired each one off with a person they did not like for some reason or another, and sent them off to find eggs, including a golden one. It worked. When the hunt was over we found that most of the people liked each other a lot better. One divorced couple got back together. Funny, how teaming up with someone for a common goal can make you see that person differently.

I also discovered an interesting fact one Easter when somehow in the rush of planning and cooking I somehow forgot to hide the eggs. But in life, the fun is in the search, even for eggs that are not hidden, and the guests had a great time, and we were forgiven, but mostly, I think, because there was a feast of fried chicken, pork chops, baked ham, pies and cakes waiting for them. People will forgive you anything if you cook them a good meal. Husbands and children, take note.

FANNIE
FLAGG'S
ORIGINAL
WHISTLE STOP
CAFE
COOKBOOK
•
166

Best Ever Coconut Cake

This is a Mr. McMichael specialty and truly the best coconut cake ever. I like to cut it into squares and ice it on all sides . . . Note: When the world comes to its senses and elects me queen, this is the cake I would LET THEM EAT!!

    ⅔   cup shortening

    2   cups sugar

    1   teaspoon vanilla extract

  2¾   cups all-purpose flour

    1   tablespoon baking powder

    ½   teaspoon salt

    1   cup water

    4   egg whites

    ½   teaspoon cream of tartar

    1   5-ounce can evaporated milk

    ⅓   cup sweetened condensed milk

    2   cups whipping cream

    ½   cup powdered sugar

    1   cup flaked coconut

Preheat oven to 350° F. In an electric mixer cream shortening and sugar; beat in vanilla. Sift together flour, baking powder, and salt and add to creamed mixture alternately with water, beginning and ending with dry ingredients. Beat egg whites and cream of tartar until stiff peaks form; fold into batter. Spoon into a greased and floured 13- × 9- × 2-inch baking pan. Bake for 30 minutes, or until a wooden pick inserted in center comes out clean. Let cool 10 minutes; remove from pan and place on a cake platter. Using a meat fork, poke holes all over surface of warm cake. Combine evaporated milk and sweetened condensed milk; spoon evenly over warm cake, allowing to soak in. Let cool to room temperature.

Beat whipping cream and powdered sugar until stiff peaks

"Evelyn had brought dyed eggs, candy corn, and Easter chocolates, and told Mrs. Threadgoode that they would celebrate all over again this week since she had not been with her on the actual day. Mrs. Threadgoode thought that was a fine idea, and told Evelyn that candy corn was her favorite and that she liked to bite the white tips off first and save the rest for later, and she proceeded to do so as she reported on Easter."

form; fold in ¾ cup coconut. Spread on cake. Sprinkle with remaining ¼ cup coconut. Refrigerate before serving, and store in refrigerator.   YIELD: 15 SERVINGS

There is nothing happier to see you than a cocker spaniel—it will just about wag its tail off—unless it's a table full of hungry people waiting on that fresh made coconut cake you are about to bring out of the kitchen . . .

Gingerbread

2¾ cups all-purpose flour
1½ teaspoons baking soda
½ teaspoon salt
1 teaspoon ground cinnamon
1½ teaspoons ground ginger
¼ teaspoon ground cloves
⅔ cup water
⅓ cup shortening, melted
1 cup molasses
1 egg beaten
Glaze (recipe follows) or Lemon Sauce (page 185)

Preheat oven to 350° F. Combine first 6 ingredients in a large bowl; mix well. Combine water, shortening, molasses, and egg. Mix well, and stir into flour mixture. Pour batter into a greased 9-inch square pan. Bake for 35 to 40 minutes, or until a wooden pick inserted in center comes out clean. Spread glaze on warm gingerbread, if desired, and serve; or serve warm with Lemon Sauce.   YIELD: 6 SERVINGS

FANNIE
FLAGG'S
ORIGINAL
WHISTLE STOP
CAFE
COOKBOOK
•
168

GLAZE

1   cup sifted powdered sugar
2   tablespoons boiling water
½   teaspoon vanilla extract

Combine all ingredients; spread on warm cake.

Attention: Can anyone explain to me why if we can go to the moon and can invent smart bombs, have the technical knowledge to blow up the world seven times over, then why in the world can't someone take the time to invent a pill that can control our metabolism so that we can eat all the good food we want and not gain weight? How hard can that be? I would rather have that extra piece of cake and pass on the smart bombs, thank you.

Hawaiian Cake

1 18.5-ounce package butter recipe golden cake
   mix
½ cup margarine, softened
⅔ cup milk
3 eggs
1 11-ounce can mandarin oranges, drained and chopped
1 3.4-ounce package vanilla instant pudding mix
1 20-ounce can crushed pineapple in heavy syrup,
   undrained
3 cups frozen thawed whipped topping or 2 cups
   whipping cream, whipped

Preheat oven to 325° F. Combine first 4 ingredients in a large mixing bowl; beat at low speed of electric mixer until blended. Beat at medium speed 3 minutes. Stir in oranges. Pour into 3 greased and floured 9-inch round cake pans; bake for 25 to 30 minutes, or until a wooden pick inserted in center comes out clean. Cool in pans 10 minutes; remove from pans and cool completely on wire racks.

Combine pudding mix and pineapple in a large bowl; mix well. Chill. Fold in whipped topping. Spread this frosting between layers and on top and sides of cake; refrigerate immediately and store in refrigerator after cutting. **YIELD: ONE 3-LAYER 9-INCH CAKE**

My advice to wives is keep your husbands a little chunky. It keeps them humble and keeps them at home. Men who go on diets have led to more divorces than you know. First, they start to lose a little weight; second, they try getting into shape. Then, pretty soon, here come the hair transplants, the contact lenses, and one morning you look up and he's heading out the door dressed in little thin

FANNIE
FLAGG'S
ORIGINAL
WHISTLE STOP
CAFE
COOKBOOK
•
170

silk running shorts, about to run in the 10K marathon that the bank is sponsoring, where he will meet the twenty-year-old blonde who thinks he's wonderful and doesn't know he snores. Mark my words: Slip him a little extra gravy . . . you'll thank me for it.

Hummingbird Cake

3	cups all-purpose flour
1½	teaspoons baking soda
½	teaspoon salt
2	cups sugar
1	teaspoon ground cinnamon
3	eggs, beaten
1¼	cups vegetable oil
2	teaspoons vanilla extract
1	8-ounce can crushed pineapple, well drained
¾	cup chopped pecans
¼	cup chopped black walnuts
2	cups chopped bananas

Cream Cheese Frosting (recipe follows)

Preheat oven to 350° F. Combine first 5 ingredients in a large bowl; add eggs, oil, and vanilla, stirring until dry ingredients are moistened. Stir in pineapple, pecans, black walnuts, and bananas. Pour into 3 greased and floured 9-inch round cake pans. Bake for 25 to 30 minutes, or until a wooden pick inserted in center comes out clean. Cool in pans 10 minutes; remove from pans, and cool on wire racks.

Spread cream cheese frosting between layers and on top and sides of cake. Refrigerate. This tastes even better the next day.

YIELD: ONE 3-LAYER 9-INCH CAKE

FANNIE
FLAGG'S
ORIGINAL
WHISTLESTOP
CAFE
COOKBOOK

•

172

CREAM CHEESE FROSTING

- ½ cup butter or margarine, softened
- 1 8-ounce package cream cheese, softened
- 1 1-pound box powdered sugar, sifted
- 2 teaspoons vanilla extract
- ½ cup finely chopped pecans (optional)

Beat butter and cream cheese until fluffy; beat in sugar and vanilla until smooth. Stir in pecans if desired. **YIELD: ENOUGH FILLING AND FROSTING FOR A 3-LAYER CAKE.**

Lane Cake

This is a true Alabama cake and was the favorite of my lifelong friend and mentor, Daddy Hatcher. Here's to you sweetheart.

- 1 cup butter or margarine, softened
- 1¾ cups sugar
- 3¼ cups all-purpose flour
- 1 tablespoon plus 1 teaspoon baking powder
- 1 teaspoon salt
- 1 cup milk
- 1½ teaspoons vanilla extract
- 8 egg whites, stiffly beaten (use yolks for filling)
- Lane Cake Filling (recipe follows)
- 1½ cups whipping cream
- ⅓ cup sifted powdered sugar
- 2 tablespoons bourbon or Jack Daniel's whiskey

Preheat oven to 325° F. Cream butter in large bowl of electric mixer; gradually add sugar, beating well. Combine flour, baking powder, and salt. Add dry ingredients to creamed mixture alternately with milk mixed with vanilla, beginning and ending with dry ingredients. Fold in egg whites. Pour batter into 3 greased and floured 9-inch round cake pans. Bake for 25 minutes, or until a wooden pick inserted in center comes out clean. Let cool in pans 10 minutes; remove from pans and cool on wire racks. Spread filling between layers and on top of cake. Beat remaining ingredients until stiff peaks form; spread on sides of cake. Store in refrigerator.   YIELD: ONE 3-LAYER 9-INCH CAKE

LANE CAKE FILLING

    8 egg yolks
 1½ cups sugar
  ½ cup butter or margarine
    1 cup chopped pecans
    1 cup frozen, thawed shredded coconut
    1 cup chopped raisins
    1 cup finely chopped maraschino cherries
  ¼ cup bourbon or Jack Daniel's whiskey

Combine first 3 ingredients in a heavy saucepan. Cook over medium heat, stirring constantly, for 15 to 20 minutes, or until thickened. Remove from heat and stir in remaining ingredients. Cool to room temperature before spreading on cake.   YIELD: ENOUGH FILLING FOR A 3-LAYER CAKE

delicate sparkle dust sprinkled on it. And if you looked inside the egg, you could see a miniature scene of a tiny little family: a mother, a father, and two little girls and a dog, standing in front of a house that looked just like ours. I could look inside that egg for hours. . . ."

Lemon-Filled Coconut Layer Cake

Batter and milk mixture for Best Ever Coconut
Cake (page 167)
1¼ cups sugar
 ¼ cup cornstarch
  1 cup plus 2 tablespoons water
  2 egg yolks, beaten
  2 tablespoons margarine
  1 tablespoon grated lemon rind
  3 tablespoons lemon juice
  2 cups whipping cream
 ½ cup powdered sugar
1¼ cups flaked coconut

Preheat oven to 350° F. Prepare batter for cake; spread in 2 greased and floured 9-inch cake pans. Bake for 25 minutes, or until a wooden pick inserted in center comes out clean. Cool in pans 10 minutes; remove from pans. Poke holes all over tops of layers; spoon milk mixture on warm layers, allowing to soak in. Let cool completely on wire racks.

Combine sugar and cornstarch in a saucepan; mix well. Stir in water until smooth, then whisk in egg yolks. Cook over medium heat until thickened and mixture just comes to a boil, stirring constantly. Remove from heat; stir in margarine, lemon rind, and lemon juice until smooth. Cool, and spread between cake layers. Beat whipping cream and powdered sugar until stiff peaks form; fold in ¾ cup coconut. Spread on top and sides of cake; sprinkle remaining ½ cup coconut on outside of cake. Refrigerate before cutting. **YIELD: ONE 2-LAYER 9-INCH CAKE**

FANNIE
FLAGG'S
ORIGINAL
WHISTLESTOP
CAFE
COOKBOOK
•
174

Mississippi Mud Cake

People in Mississippi say, It ain't Mississippi mud if it doesn't leave your mouth coated with sugar.

1¼   cups all-purpose flour
  2   teaspoons baking powder
  ½   teaspoon salt
  2   cups sugar
  ¾   cup unsweetened cocoa
  5   eggs, separated
  1   cup water
  1   teaspoon vanilla extract
2½   cups miniature marshmallows
Mud Icing (recipe follows)

Preheat oven to 350° F. Sift flour, baking powder, and salt together 3 times. Set aside. Combine sugar and cocoa; mix well. Beat egg yolks in large bowl of electric mixer. Beat in water, vanilla, and sugar mixture at medium speed. Beat in flour mixture. Beat egg whites until stiff peaks form; stir one-fourth of chocolate batter gently into whites. Fold egg whites into remaining batter. Pour into a greased and floured 13- × 9- × 2-inch baking pan and bake for 25 to 30 minutes, or until a wooden pick inserted in center comes out clean. Remove from oven and sprinkle marshmallows evenly over cake. Bake 5 minutes longer, or until marshmallows begin to melt. Cool in pan on a wire rack. Spread with mud icing.   **YIELD: 15 SERVINGS**

MUD ICING

  1 cup butter or margarine, melted
 ⅓ cup unsweetened cocoa
 ½ cup evaporated milk
  4 cups sifted powdered sugar
  1 teaspoon vanilla extract
 ½ cup chopped pecans (optional)

Combine butter and cocoa in a large mixing bowl; stir in evaporated milk. Gradually beat in sugar and vanilla until smooth. Stir in pecans. **YIELD: ENOUGH FROSTING FOR ONE 13- × 9- × 2-INCH CAKE**

Red Velvet Cake

  1 teaspoon baking soda
  1 tablespoon vinegar
 ½ cup shortening
1½ cups sugar
  2 eggs
  2 cups all-purpose flour
  1 tablespoon unsweetened cocoa
 ½ teaspoon salt
  1 cup buttermilk
  1 teaspoon vanilla extract
  2 ounces red food coloring
Custard Frosting (recipe follows)
Flaked coconut (optional)

Preheat oven to 350° F. Dissolve soda in vinegar; set aside. Cream shortening, add sugar, and beat well with electric mixer. Add eggs, one at a time, beating well after each addition. Beat in soda mixture.

FANNIE
FLAGG'S
ORIGINAL
WHISTLE STOP
CAFE
COOKBOOK
•
176

Sift together flour, cocoa, and salt. Combine buttermilk, vanilla, and food coloring. Add dry ingredients to creamed mixture alternately with buttermilk mixture, beginning and ending with flour mixture. Pour batter into 2 greased and floured 9-inch round cake pans. Bake for 25 to 35 minutes, or until a wooden pick inserted in center comes out clean. Cool in pans 10 minutes; remove from pans and cool completely on wire racks. Spread custard frosting between layers and on top and sides of cake; sprinkle with coconut if desired.   YIELD: ONE 2-LAYER 9-INCH CAKE

CUSTARD FROSTING

The 1½ cups sugar is not a typo; this is not a very sweet frosting but perfectly complements the cake.

>   1   cup milk
> ¼   cup all-purpose flour
> ⅛   teaspoon salt
> ½   cup shortening
> ½   cup butter or margarine
> 1½   cups sifted powdered sugar
>   1   teaspoon vanilla extract

Combine milk, flour, and salt in a small saucepan; stir until smooth, using a wire whisk. Cook over medium heat, stirring constantly until thickened. Cool completely.

Cream shortening and butter; beat in powdered sugar and vanilla until smooth. Beat in milk mixture.   YIELD: ENOUGH FROSTING AND FILLING FOR A 2-LAYER CAKE

Puddings, Ice Cream, and Custards

FANNIE
FLAGG'S
ORIGINAL
WHISTLE STOP
CAFE
COOKBOOK

•

178

Boiled Custard

Boiled custard should be "coddled" so the eggs don't overcook and make the mixture lumpy. Here's a tip: If it ever does lump on you from too high heat or whatever, press the cooked mixture through a sieve and it's as good as cooked right. If you add more flour to a boiled custard, it becomes creamier and less eggy tasting. I've shown how by adding more flour to the boiled custard and added a few flavor variations.

> 1 cup sugar
> 1 tablespoon all-purpose flour
> 4 large eggs, beaten
> 1 quart whole milk
> 1½ teaspoons vanilla extract
> Ground nutmeg

Combine sugar and flour in a heavy medium saucepan. Combine eggs and milk in a bowl; beat until blended using a wire whisk. Gradually stir into saucepan, stirring until smooth. Cook over medium heat, stirring constantly, until thickened enough to coat a metal spoon. Do not boil. Remove from heat, and stir in vanilla. Place a piece of heavy-duty plastic wrap directly on surface of custard to keep it from forming a skin; cool to room temperature. Pour into individual serving dishes or one large one; sprinkle with nutmeg. Cover and refrigerate until set.   **YIELD: 6 TO 8 SERVINGS**

VANILLA PUDDING: Increase flour to ¼ cup, and proceed as directed above.

CHOCOLATE PUDDING: Increase flour to 3 tablespoons; add 1 cup semisweet chocolate chips to milk mixture before cooking, and proceed as directed above.

"One time, they had this raccoon named Cookie, and I used to spend hours watching him try to wash a cracker. They'd put a little pan of water out in the backyard, and then they'd give him a soda cracker, and he'd wash cracker after cracker, and never could figure out what happened to it when it would disappear. Each time, he'd look at his little empty hands and be so surprised. He'd wash cookies, too, but that wasn't as funny . . . he washed an ice cream cone once . . ."

BUTTERSCOTCH PUDDING: Increase flour to 3 tablespoons; add 1 cup butterscotch chips to milk mixture before cooking, and proceed as directed above.

COCONUT PUDDING: Increase flour to ¼ cup; proceed as directed above. Add 1 teaspoon coconut extract with vanilla extract; stir ½ to 1 cup flaked coconut into hot pudding mixture.

Cholesterol . . . isn't that a seasoning?

Vanilla Custard Ice Cream

        4   cups milk
     2¼   cups sugar
        ¼   cup all-purpose flour
        ¼   teaspoon salt
        6   eggs, beaten
        4   cups half-and-half
        1   tablespoon vanilla extract
        1   whole vanilla bean, split and scraped

Heat milk in a 3-quart saucepan over low heat until hot. Combine sugar, flour, and salt; gradually add sugar mixture to milk, stirring until smooth. Cook over medium heat until thickened, stirring constantly. Gradually stir about one-fourth of milk mixture into beaten eggs; add to remaining milk mixture, stirring constantly. Cook 1 minute. Remove from heat and let cool. Cover and chill at least 2 hours. Combine the half-and-half, vanilla extract, and vanilla bean in a large bowl; add chilled custard, whisking until blended. Pour into freezer can of a 1-gallon hand-turned or electric ice cream freezer. Freeze according to manufacturer's instructions. Let ripen 1½ to 2 hours.
YIELD: 1 GALLON.

FANNIE
FLAGG'S
ORIGINAL
WHISTLE STOP
CAFE
COOKBOOK
•
180

VARIATION: STRAWBERRY OR PEACH ICE CREAM: Combine 3 cups chopped or mashed strawberries or peaches and ¼ cup sugar; let stand 1 hour. Add to ice cream cannister when ice cream begins to harden.

VARIATION: CHOCOLATE CHIP ICE CREAM: Add one 4-ounce bar finely chopped semisweet or German sweet baking chocolate to ice cream cannister when ice cream begins to harden.

Aren't people lucky? I mean, who else on this earth gets to eat a bowl of freshly made hot peach cobbler with a scoop of cold, creamy vanilla ice cream on the side while surrounded by people you love and who love you?

Banana Pudding

If you are mad at somebody give them a bowl of this pudding . . . on second thought, have a bowl yourself! Then you will both feel better.

3	cups sugar
½	cup all-purpose flour
¼	cup cornstarch
6	eggs, separated, plus 2 egg yolks
7	cups milk
¼	cup margarine
2	teaspoons vanilla extract
1	16-ounce box vanilla wafers, or one and a half 12-ounce boxes
10	to 12 medium bananas, peeled and sliced

"Evelyn had brought an assortment of cookies from the Nabisco company, hoping to cheer her mother-in-law up, but Big Mama had said no thank you, that she didn't care for any, so Evelyn took them down the hall to Mrs. Threadgoode, who was delighted. 'I could eat ginger snaps and vanilla wafers all day long, couldn't you?'

Evelyn unfortunately had to nod yes."

Thoroughly mix 2½ cups of the sugar, the flour, and corn-starch in a large heavy saucepan. Lightly beat the 8 egg yolks; combine milk and egg yolks and whisk into sugar mixture. Add margarine and cook over medium heat, stirring constantly, until mixture is thickened. Remove from heat; stir in 1 teaspoon of the vanilla. Cool. Preheat oven to 425° F. Line bottom of a 13- × 9- × 2-inch baking dish with one-third of vanilla wafers; layer one-third of bananas and one-third of custard on top. Repeat layers twice. Beat egg whites until foamy; gradually add remaining ½ cup sugar, 1 tablespoon at a time, beating until stiff peaks form. Beat in remaining 1 teaspoon vanilla. Spread over custard, seal-ing to edges. Bake for 10 minutes, or until lightly browned. Chill overnight before serving.   **YIELD: 12 SERVINGS**

NOTE: Whipped topping or whipped cream may be spread over pudding instead of meringue, if desired. In this case, obviously, you don't bake it.

NOTE: This makes a huge pan of pudding. But it is certainly better after a few days of sitting, and if you go to the trouble to make your own custard, which is the key to great banana pudding, by the way, you might as well double the recipe and make a big pan.

FANNIE
FLAGG'S
ORIGINAL
WHISTLE STOP
CAFE
COOKBOOK
•
182

Bread Pudding

You may use raisins if you wish but be sure to soak them in bourbon overnight . . . better yet, throw the raisins away and drink the bourbon.

   1   cup raisins (if you must)
  ½   cup bourbon
   6   cups coarsely crumbled biscuits or cubed bread
   2   cups half-and-half
1½   cups milk
   3   eggs plus 1 egg white, slightly beaten
   1   tablespoon vanilla extract
1½   cups sugar
  ½   teaspoon ground cinnamon
  ¼   cup butter or margarine, melted

Soak raisins in bourbon overnight. Preheat oven to 325° F. Place biscuits in a large bowl and pour half-and-half and milk over them. Let stand 10 minutes, then crush with hands until blended. Add eggs and egg white, and vanilla; mix well. Combine sugar and cinnamon; add to biscuit mixture, and stir in raisin mixture. Pour melted butter in a 13- × 9- × 2-inch baking pan; spoon pudding mixture into pan. Bake for 30 minutes, or until very firm. Cool; cut into squares and pour Lemon Custard Sauce (page 185) or Lemon Sauce (page 185) over.   **YIELD: 12 TO 15 SERVINGS**

Rice Pudding

Show me a person who doesn't like rice pudding, and I'll bet after they eat this one, you will have a rice pudding convert.

⅔ cup long-grain (not converted) rice
3 cups milk
1 2-inch piece vanilla bean
1¼ cups sugar
2 tablespoons butter
½ teaspoon salt
4 eggs, separated

Combine rice and milk in top of a double boiler. Cook, covered, over simmering water for 30 minutes, or until rice is just tender.

Preheat oven to 350° F. Split vanilla bean lengthwise and scrape out seeds. Combine ¾ cup sugar and vanilla bean seeds in a food processor fitted with steel blade and process until finely ground almost to a powder. Stir sugar mixture, butter, salt, and beaten egg yolks into warm rice mixture; mix well. Pour pudding into a greased, shallow 1½-quart baking dish. Bake for 30 minutes or until custard is not quite set. Remove from oven and let cool on a wire rack 10 minutes. As pudding is cooling, beat egg whites until foamy; gradually add remaining ½ cup sugar, 1 tablespoon at a time, beating until stiff peaks form. Spread gently over pudding, and continue baking 15 to 20 minutes longer, or until meringue is light brown. Serve warm. **YIELD: 6 SERVINGS**

NOTE: To make a real boiled old-fashioned custard or to cook milk, do it gently over boiling water so the mixture doesn't come in contact with direct heat and the egg proteins don't coagulate and lump.

FANNIE
FLAGG'S
ORIGINAL
WHISTLESTOP
CAFE
COOKBOOK
•
184

Lemon Custard Sauce

½ cup sugar
¼ cup all-purpose flour
⅛ teaspoon salt
1½ cups milk
4 egg yolks, beaten
¼ cup fresh lemon juice

Combine sugar, flour, and salt in a small saucepan; mix well. Beat together milk and egg yolks; stir into sugar mixture. Cook over medium heat, stirring constantly, until thickened and mixture just comes to a boil. Remove from heat and stir in lemon juice. Serve warm.   **YIELD: 2 CUPS**

Lemon Sauce

This just makes everything better! Except rutabaga.

½ cup sugar
1½ tablespoons all-purpose flour
1 cup water
3 tablespoons fresh lemon juice
Pinch of salt
2 tablespoons butter, cut into pieces and softened

Combine sugar and flour in a small saucepan; mix well. Stir in water, lemon juice, and salt until smooth. Bring to a boil over medium heat, stirring constantly until sugar melts. Reduce heat, and boil gently 1 minute. Remove from heat and whisk in butter, 1 tablespoon at a time. Serve warm or at room temperature.
YIELD: 1½ CUPS

Strawberry Shortcakes

I look for small, dark strawberries. They are the tastiest.

  6 to 8 cups sliced strawberries
  ½ plus ⅓ cup sugar, plus more for sprinkling
  2½ cups all-purpose flour
  ¾ cup cake flour
  2 tablespoons baking powder
  ¾ teaspoon salt
  1 cup butter or margarine, chilled and cut into
      pieces
  ¾ to 1 cup milk
  1 egg
  1 tablespoon water
  Whipped cream

Combine strawberries and ½ cup sugar. Toss and let stand at room temperature 2 hours. Preheat oven to 425° F. Combine ⅓ cup sugar with next 4 ingredients in a large bowl; cut in butter with a pastry blender until mixture resembles coarse meal. Add ¾ cup milk and mix with a fork just until dough holds together, adding more milk if needed. Dough should be soft. Turn dough out onto a floured surface and knead gently 8 to 10 times. Pat it out ¾ inch thick and cut into rounds, using a 2½-inch biscuit cutter. Place on a greased baking sheet. Combine egg and water, beating well; brush on tops of biscuits. Sprinkle with sugar. Bake for 12 to 15 minutes, or until lightly browned. Split and serve with strawberries and whipped cream. **YIELD: 10 SERVINGS**

Peach (or Apple) Cobbler

2 cups all-purpose flour
1 teaspoon baking powder
¾ teaspoon salt
3 tablespoons sugar
¼ cup shortening
¾ cup whipping cream
8 cups sliced fresh peaches or apples
2 cups sugar, plus more for sprinkling
2 tablespoons all-purpose flour
½ teaspoon ground cinnamon
1 teaspoon vanilla extract
⅓ cup butter or margarine

Combine first 4 ingredients; cut in shortening until mixture resembles coarse meal. Sprinkle cream over mixture and toss with fork until dough forms a ball. Knead 4 or 5 times; wrap in plastic wrap, and chill at least 1 hour. Meanwhile, combine fruit, 2 cups sugar, flour, and cinnamon in a dutch oven; set aside until syrup forms. Bring to a boil; reduce heat, and simmer, uncovered, 10 minutes or until tender. Remove from heat, and stir in vanilla and butter until melted. Preheat oven to 475° F. Roll half of pastry to a 12- × 8- inch rectangle. Spoon half of fruit into a lightly buttered 12- × 8- × 2-inch baking dish; place pastry on top. Sprinkle with a little sugar; bake for 15 minutes, or until very lightly browned. Spoon remaining fruit on top; roll remaining pastry to ⅛-inch thickness and cut into 1-inch strips. Arrange strips in lattice design over peaches. Sprinkle with sugar. Bake 20 additional minutes or until browned. **YIELD: 8 TO 10 SERVINGS**

FANNIE
FLAGG'S
ORIGINAL
WHISTLE STOP
CAFE
COOKBOOK
•
188

Ambrosia

After a heavy meal this is a refreshing treat. I like it after Christmas dinner. Sectioning and peeling the oranges is a pain, but the results are well worth it.

12 large seedless oranges, peeled and sectioned
1 pound frozen sweetened coconut, thawed
½ cup sugar

Cut orange sections in half; combine all ingredients in a large serving bowl. Cover and refrigerate overnight.   **YIELD: 10 TO 12 SERVINGS**

Special Ambrosia

Serve with pound cake or angel food cake for sopping up the juices.

1 20-ounce can pineapple tidbits, undrained
1 pound frozen shredded coconut, thawed
⅔ cup sugar
4 or 5 large oranges, peeled and sectioned
2 large or 3 medium bananas, sliced

Drain pineapple, reserving juice. Measure out and reserve 2 tablespoons coconut; combine remaining coconut and sugar and mix well. Layer half of orange sections, bananas, pineapple, and coconut mixture in a glass serving bowl. Repeat layers. Drizzle pineapple juice over top; sprinkle with reserved coconut. Cover and refrigerate overnight.   **YIELD: 10 SERVINGS**

Jams, Jellies, Condiments

The Well-Laid Table

The correct table setting in a cafe starts with thinking of catsup as a centerpiece. A good cafe table will include a bottle of catsup, a jar of mustard, steak sauce, Worcestershire sauce, large salt and pepper shakers, and plastic flowers, faded yellow if possible. Depending on how far south you go and how popular the turnip greens, you will notice that something else starts showing up: *pepper sauce*.

It comes in a variety of slender, clear glass bottles containing tiny little red and green peppers in vinegar. These cylinders of peppers have been there as long as the cafe. The vinegar is replaced as needed and the same peppers are used over and over. Pepper sauce is a must for greens, good for all greens, and it will even perk up the spirits of spinach. A good jar of pepper sauce will be handed down for generations. Many a bride receives the family jar of pepper sauce to set proudly on her table, and points to it with pride. "Yes, that's grandmother Thomas on my mother's side's pepper sauce. I'm saving it for my little girl. . . . Try it, you'll like it."

FANNIE
FLAGG'S
ORIGINAL
WHISTLESTOP
CAFE
COOKBOOK
•
192

Cinnamon Peach Preserves

This has a bite, but I like to make it at times without the cinnamon, just plain.

2 pounds fresh peaches, peeled and thickly sliced
3 cups sugar
1 cup honey
½ cup water
2 3-inch pieces stick cinnamon

Combine peaches, 1½ cups sugar, honey, water, and cinnamon in a dutch oven. Bring to a boil, stirring constantly until sugar melts. Reduce heat and simmer 15 minutes, stirring frequently. Remove from heat; let stand 1 hour. Add remaining 1½ cups sugar and bring to a rapid boil, stirring constantly until sugar melts. Boil, uncovered, until mixture registers 221° F. on a candy thermometer, stirring frequently. Remove from heat; skim off foam and remove cinnamon sticks. Immediately spoon into hot sterilized jars, leaving ¼-inch headspace. Wipe jar rims, cover with metal lids, and screw on bands. Process in boiling water bath for 15 minutes. **YIELD: 3 TO 4 HALF-PINTS**

"There was only about four tables and a bunch of uncertain chairs," she laughed. 'You never know for certain if they was gonna hold you up or not. And they never did have a cash register. They just kept the money in a Roy Tan Cigar box and made your change out of that. At the counter they had potato chips and pig skins on a rack, combs and chewin' tobacco, fishing lures and little corncob pipes.'

"Idgie opened the place at daybreak and didn't close the place until, as she said, 'the last dog was hung.'"

Easy Sweet Delicious Strawberry Preserves

Strawberry perserves on hot biscuits . . . oh my . . .

    2 pints strawberries, hulled
    3 cups sugar

    Combine berries and 1½ cups sugar in a heavy saucepan; bring to a boil, stirring constantly. Boil, uncovered 10 minutes. Add remaining sugar and boil 15 minutes, stirring frequently, until mixture reaches 221° F. on a candy thermometer. Skim foam. Cool, cover, and let stand at room temperature for 24 hours, stirring occasionally. Spoon into clean jars and refrigerate.
YIELD: 3 HALF-PINTS

Mother always said, "if you can't say something nice, don't say anything." Just think, if everyone followed her advice, there would be no newspapers, television news programs or critics. Not a bad thought after all.

Muscadine Jam

Muscadine grapes are sweet to eat and pretty to look at as well.

    4 pounds muscadine grapes
    2 cups purple grape juice
    1 3-inch stick cinnamon
    1 1¾-ounce package powdered fruit pectin
 7¾ cups sugar

FANNIE
FLAGG'S
ORIGINAL
WHISTLESTOP
CAFE
COOKBOOK
•
194

Remove and discard stems from muscadines. Pop pulp from skins and reserve skins and pulp separately. Combine pulp and 1 cup grape juice in a dutch oven. Bring to a boil; cover, reduce heat, and simmer 5 minutes. Press mixture through a fine meshed sieve. Transfer pulp to a food processor fitted with steel blade, discarding seeds.

Place reserved skins in dutch oven; add remaining 1 cup grape juice and enough water to cover. Add cinnamon stick. Bring to a boil, cover, reduce heat, and simmer 10 minutes, or until tender. Drain, reserving liquid. Add skins to food processor, and pulse mixture in food processor until skins are very finely minced (almost ground). Discard cinnamon stick.

Measure 6 cups pulp mixture, adding reserved liquid from boiling skins if necessary to make 6 cups. Return to dutch oven. Stir in powdered fruit pectin, mixing well. Bring to a rolling boil, stirring constantly. Add sugar; return to rolling boil, stirring constantly. Boil 1 minute, stirring constantly. Remove from heat and skim off foam. Stir for 5 minutes.

Immediately spoon hot mixture into hot sterilized jars, leaving ¼-inch headspace; wipe jar rims. Cover jars at once with metal lids, and screw on metal bands. Process in boiling water bath for 15 minutes. **YIELD: 5 PINTS**

I am so lucky that the McMichaels were happy to share their recipes with me for this book. That is not always the case, however. Some people can be as stingy with their "receipts" as if they were for nuclear weapons rather than the nuclear family, and are terrified to let the secret ingredients be known. "Why yes, Aunt Baby died, clutching her famous tea cake receipt to her breast, so we just had to bury her with it." I have a vision of Aunt Baby greeting her loved ones in heaven by running to the great celestial stove in the sky and whipping up a batch of her tea cake for their first dinner in heaven. I would rather we had a chance to eat it right here and now, thank you.

Pepper Jelly

Use sweet red peppers and red food coloring if you prefer red color. This is so good on toast or biscuits. I like it with cream cheese and crackers too.

    4   to 6 green peppers
    6   to 10 hot peppers
    6   cups sugar
    1⅓ cups vinegar (5% acidity)
    2   3-ounce packages liquid pectin
    2   drops green food coloring (optional)

Wash peppers, remove seeds and ribs, and cut into chunks. Process each type of pepper, in batches, in a food processor until coarsely ground. Remove from processor, and measure. You need 1 cup ground green pepper and ⅓ cup ground hot pepper.

Combine ground peppers, sugar, and vinegar in a large saucepan; bring to a boil. Boil 6 minutes, stirring frequently. Stir in pectin; boil 3 minutes, stirring frequently. Remove from heat; skim off foam.

Quickly pour hot jelly into hot sterilized jars, leaving ¼-inch headspace; wipe jar rims clean. Cover with metal lids and screw on bands. Process in boiling water bath for 5 minutes. **YIELD: 6 HALF-PINTS**

FANNIE
FLAGG'S
ORIGINAL
WHISTLESTOP
CAFE
COOKBOOK
•
196

Refrigerator Pickles

The best place to soak these pickles is in the sink. To drain them, all you have to do is pull the plug; to rinse them just turn on the water.

2½	pounds cucumbers, peeled
2	large white onions, peeled
2	large sweet red peppers, seeded and cored
1	small head cauliflower, cut into florets
½	pound carrots, peeled
½	pound celery
½	cup pickling salt
1	bag ice
4	cups cider vinegar
4	cups sugar
1	tablespoon plus 1 teaspoon mustard seed
2	teaspoons celery seed
2	teaspoons ground turmeric
2	teaspoons red pepper flakes

Cut vegetables into ½-inch pieces. Place in a large stockpot or clean dishpan. Cover vegetables with pickling salt, then ice. Let stand 24 hours, adding ice when needed. When ready to cook, rinse vegetables in cold water, and drain.

Combine remaining ingredients in a large dutch oven or stockpot; bring to a boil, stirring constantly. Pack vegetables in clean jars and cover with hot liquid. Store in refrigerator for 3 weeks before eating. **YIELD: ABOUT 5 QUARTS**

Pickled Okra

  5 hot red peppers
  5 cloves garlic, peeled and halved
3½ pounds small okra pods
  1 tablespoon plus 2 teaspoons dillseed or dillweed
  4 cups water
  2 cups distilled white vinegar
 ⅓ cup salt

Place 1 hot pepper and 2 garlic halves in each of 5 hot sterile pint jars. Trim tough stems from okra pods; pack okra tightly into jars. Add 1 teaspoon dill to each jar. Combine remaining ingredients in a saucepan and bring to a boil. Reduce heat and simmer 5 minutes. Pour over okra, leaving ¼-inch headspace. Remove air bubbles; wipe jar rims. Cover at once with metal lids, and screw on bands. Process in boiling water bath for 10 minutes. Let jars stand in a cool, dark place for several weeks before opening. **YIELD: 5 PINTS**

FANNIE
FLAGG'S
ORIGINAL
WHISTLESTOP
CAFE
COOKBOOK
•
198

Old-Fashioned Corn Relish

½ cup cider vinegar

¼ cup sugar

½ teaspoon salt

½ teaspoon celery seed

¼ teaspoon mustard seed

¼ teaspoon hot sauce

1 12-ounce can whole kernel corn, drained

2 tablespoons minced green pepper

1 tablespoon chopped drained pimiento

1 tablespoon minced onion

Combine first 5 ingredients in a small saucepan; bring to a
boil, stirring constantly until sugar melts. Reduce heat and simmer, uncovered, for 2 minutes. Remove from heat; stir in hot
sauce, corn, green pepper, pimiento, and onion. Transfer to a
bowl; cover and chill.   **YIELD: 1⅔ CUPS**

Cranberry Orange Relish

5 cups fresh or frozen thawed cranberries

2 cups sugar

1 cup orange juice

½ cup finely chopped orange rind

½ teaspoon ground nutmeg

½ teaspoon ground cardamom

Combine all ingredients in a heavy saucepan; stir well. Bring
to a boil, stirring constantly until sugar melts. Reduce heat and
simmer, uncovered, for 10 minutes or until cranberries pop, stirring occasionally. Remove from heat; cool. Transfer to a serving
bowl and chill.   **YIELD: 4 CUPS**

Spicy Green
Tomato Chutney

    2 pounds firm green tomatoes, cored and cut into
       ½-inch slices
    2 large green cooking apples (1 pound), peeled, cored,
       and diced
    ½ pound tiny pickling onions, peeled
    1 cup firmly packed dark brown sugar
    ½ cup raisins
 1½ tablespoons minced crystallized ginger
    2 teaspoons crushed red pepper
    3 cloves garlic, peeled and minced
 1¼ cups cider vinegar

Combine all ingredients in a large, heavy stockpot or dutch oven, stirring well. Bring to a boil; reduce heat, and simmer for 50 minutes or until very thick, stirring frequently.

Ladle into hot sterilized jars, leaving ½-inch headspace. Cover at once with metal lids, and screw bands tight. Process relish in boiling water bath for 15 minutes.   **YIELD: 5 HALF-PINTS**

FANNIE
FLAGG'S
ORIGINAL
WHISTLESTOP
CAFE
COOKBOOK
•
200

Drinks: An Ode to Grapico

Drinks are very popular down South because it's so hot and we love a sweet drink of any kind, and also it is very sociable. You never go into anyone's home without being offered a cold drink of some kind. Everybody loves iced tea and we drink gallons of it, but other cold drinks are popular too, and certain drinks go with certain food. As I'll say more than once, nothing is better with barbecue than a big ole bottle of ice cold orange crush, or a bottle of Grapico. As a child, I used to love Grapicos. The bottle seemed so big that I could hardly get my hands around it, it turned your mouth and lips a bright purple, and was so sweet that it made your hair stand up on your head. My, but it was good.

Plain Cokes or Dr. Pepper or R.C. Cola are best with hot dogs, hamburgers, and all sandwiches, but in the South the very best drink on a hot summer afternoon was a large frosty glass of creamy vanilla ice cream with golden Buffalo Rock Ginger Ale poured on top. Buffalo Rock Ginger Ale advertised that it had been "mellowed a million moments or more." I don't understand how people can eat a meal without having something good like iced tea or a Coke to go with it. The fad in California is to drink designer water, Evian, Perrier, or the like, with meals. When I took one of my California friends to a cafe in Alabama, she asked, before ordering her food, what kind of water they served. The waitress looked at her and thought for a moment and said, "Hydrant."

FANNIE
FLAGG'S
ORIGINAL
WHISTLE STOP
CAFE
COOKBOOK

•

202

"They drove back over the tracks, and Mrs. Hartman said, 'Honey, if you take a right on the next street, I'll show you where the old Threadgoode place is.'

The minute they turned the corner, she saw it: a big, two-story white wooden house with the front porch that went all around. She recognized it from the pictures.

Evelyn pulled up in front, and they got out.

The windows were mostly broken and boarded up, and the wood on the front porch was caved in and rotten, so they couldn't go up. It looked like the whole house was ready to fall down. They walked around to the back.

Evelyn said, 'What a shame they let this place go. I'll bet it was beautiful at one time.'

Mrs. Hartman agreed. 'At one time, this was the prettiest house in Whistle Stop. But all the Threadgoodes are gone now, so I guess they're just gonna tear it down one of these days.'

When they got to the backyard, Evelyn and Mrs. Hartman were surprised at what they saw. The old trellis, leaning on the back of the house, was entirely covered with thousands of little pink sweetheart roses, blooming like they had no idea that the people inside had left long ago.

Evelyn peeked in the broken window and saw a cracked, white enamel table. She wondered how many biscuits had been cut on that table throughout the years.

Although it was late, Evelyn decided to drive by the old house one more time. It was just getting dark, and as she came down the street, her lights hit the windows in such a way that it looked to her like there were people inside, moving around . . . and all of a sudden, she could have sworn that she heard Essie Rue pounding away at the old piano in the parlor . . .

'Buffalo gals, won't you come out tonight, come out tonight . . .'

Evelyn stopped the car and sat there, sobbing like her heart would break, wondering why people had to get old and die."

"*N*ow that I look back, it seems to me that after the cafe closed, the heart of the town just stopped beating. Funny how a little knockabout place like that brought so many people together."

FANNIE
FLAGG'S
ORIGINAL
WHISTLE STOP
CAFE
COOKBOOK
•
204

Index

Photo Credits

About the Author

*Y*ou might think Fannie Flagg first came to public attention when she knocked 'em dead in the Miss Alabama contest by modeling a dress she had designed herself, made entirely out of old menus. ("I've *always* been fascinated with food," she says.) Or later, when she went on to become a remarkably successful actress, novelist, and screenwriter. She has appeared on television, in movies, and starred on the Broadway stage. *Daisy Fay and the Miracle Man*, her first novel, was critically acclaimed and was chosen by the Book-of-the-Month Club. Her second novel, *Fried Green Tomatoes at the Whistle Stop Cafe*, was a New York Times bestseller. She received the prestigious Scripters Award and was nominated for both the Writers Guild of America and an Academy Award for her screenplay of the movie *Fried Green Tomatoes* starring Jessica Tandy and Kathy Bates.

But in fact she was first seen in public as a beautiful smiling child, buddying up to a bottle of Orange Crush bigger than she was and looking out cheerfully over a plate of hot, delicious barbecue in a certain little cafe down south.